Travellers in History Series

LOUIS SIMOND

An American in Regency England

Travellers in History Series

LOUIS SIMOND

An American in Regency England

THE JOURNAL OF A TOUR IN 1810–1811

*Edited with an Introduction
and notes by*
CHRISTOPHER HIBBERT

Robert Maxwell
LONDON

Copyright © 1968 Pergamon Press Ltd.
First published by Robert Maxwell: Publisher
4 Fitzroy Square, London, W.1.
A division of Pergamon Press Ltd.
Library of Congress Catalog Card No. 68-22076

Printed and bound in Great Britain by
Hazell Watson & Viney Ltd.
Aylesbury, Bucks

08 007074 4

Contents

INTRODUCTION 7

1. Falmouth to London, 24 December 1809–
   8 January 1810   11
2. London, 11 January 1810–4 June 1810   23
3. East Anglia, the West Country and Wales,
   12 June 1810–2 August 1810   55
4. Scotland, 2 August 1810–20 February 1811   73
5. The North and the Midlands, 27 February 1811–
   24 March 1811   101
6. London, 25 March 1811–25 September 1811   125

INDEX   169

Introduction

THE AUTHOR of this journal landed in Falmouth from New York on Christmas Eve 1809; he set sail on his return journey—which was to last for fifty-seven days—from Liverpool at the end of September 1811. During these twenty-one months he made as extensive a tour of England, Scotland and Wales as any foreign visitor of the time. He travelled in the West Country and in East Anglia, to Oxford and Cambridge, Chester and Bath, in the Welsh hills and the highlands of Scotland; he talked to gardeners and maidservants, lawyers and turnkeys, he met Walter Scott in Edinburgh, Sydney Smith in Yorkshire and saw George III on the terrace at Windsor, a pathetic, stooping figure with a hat flapping over his eyes, talking continually in a loud and earnest voice. He witnessed criminal trials and prize-fights, balloon ascents at Hackney and riots in Westminster; he visited numerous country houses from Blenheim to Chatsworth, from Wilton to Petworth; he went over an iron-works at Swansea, down a coal mine at Newcastle, into a Quaker lunatic asylum in York, a prison at Chester, and a hospital in London; and everywhere he went he took his journal with him, recording the kind of details which bring the period vividly to life.

In London, where he spent over six months, he comments on politics and table manners, cart-horses and the price of houses, pastry cook-shops and the smoke-laden air of the streets. He had opinions on everything and the ability to express them well. In the House of Commons he saw "a little man, as thin as a shadow, and drawing one side of his body after him, as if paralytic, hurry across the floor with a tottering brisk step and an awkward bow.... This was Mr Wilberforce. Nothing can surpass the meanness of his appearance and he seems half blind". In Newgate he watched a prisoner, convicted of attempted regicide, "picking his teeth in a corner very composedly", and "the transportation ladies, crowded in a small court, much more disorderly than the men. They threatened and wrangled among themselves, singing, vociferating, and, as much as the narrow space allowed, moving about in all sorts of dresses—one of them in men's clothes". One day he went to the British Museum and was appalled by the way the visitors were rushed round the exhibits—"many of them seemingly in a state of decay"—by a German guide of astonishing vulgarity and impudence; another day he visited Covent Garden where Mrs Siddons —"appearing still young and handsome" at fifty-five—made the whole house cry.

The journal is full of such sketches and vignettes as these; and while it adds little new to our knowledge of Regency England, it surely deserves to be recognised as one of the most evocative portraits of Britain and the British to have been drawn by a foreigner during the years of the Napoleonic Wars.

It was first published in London in 1815 under the title of *Journal of a Tour and Residence in Great Britain during the Years 1810 and 1811 by a Native of France with Remarks on the Country, its Arts, Literature, and Politics, and on the Manners and Customs of its Inhabitants*. Its anonymous author was Louis Simond who was born in Lyon in 1767 into a well-to-do Protestant family which claimed connection with the Sismondis of Pisa. Shortly before the outbreak of the French Revolution he emigrated to the United States of America where he soon established himself in a good way of business as a ship owner, and married an English wife—the "F" of his journal—a niece of John Wilkes.

During their tour of Britain, Mr and Mrs Simond were introduced to Mrs Grant of Laggan who described the wife as "the plainest, worst-dressed woman" she had ever seen, and the husband as "a dark, gloomy-looking man". They both, however, improved upon acquaintance. She turned out to be much more interesting than she appeared, while he "reserved, fastidious and philosophic in the highest sense of the phrase" was evidently a man of "talent, great refinement and agreeable conversation".

Introduction 9

After his tour of Britain he returned to America in 1811 but later came back to England where he lived until the war was over and Louis XVIII was returned to the throne of France. Following the success of this book—which, translated by himself, appeared in a French edition in 1817—Simond published two further travel books, *Voyage en Suisse* (1822) and *Voyage en Italie et en Sicile* (1827). He died in Geneva on 1 July 1831.

In preparing this edition of his English journal I have reduced its length by cutting out various passages which would not be of particular interest to the modern reader. Otherwise—except for the deletion of hundreds of commas—I have left the original text untouched. Any additions which it has been necessary to make for the sake of clarity, or for the identification of people to whom Simond refers by initials only, have been placed between square brackets.

For their expert help in providing me with various pieces of information contained in the notes I am most grateful to Miss Mary Cosh, Mrs Joan St George Saunders, the Countess of Sutherland, Mr Robin Adam, Major E. R. F. Compton, Lord Egremont, Mr Edward Hibbert, the Earl of Pembroke and Mr George Walker. I am most grateful, also, to my wife for having read the proofs and prepared the index and to Mr Gordon Grimley who is responsible for the selection of Simond's journal as the first of an interesting series.

CHRISTOPHER HIBBERT

1

FALMOUTH TO LONDON
24 December 1809 – 8 January 1810

WE FOUND ourselves, on waking this morning early, anchored in the harbour of Falmouth, where we had arrived in the night, after a speedy and prosperous passage of twenty-one days from America, without a single storm to describe, or any extraordinary occurrence. This harbour is a small basin, surrounded with gentle hills. Looking round, we saw green fields, with cattle grazing—a grove of trees—some pines, and many green tufts like laurels. The town of Falmouth—little, old, and ugly—was seen on our left, and another assemblage of little old houses on our right, (Flushing); Pendennis Castle behind us, on a mound near the entrance of the harbour. The air was calm and mild—the sky of a very pale blue—a light mist hung over the landscape—and the general impression was peaceful and agreeable: on the surface of the water twenty or thirty ships, mostly packets, and two or three Dutch vessels with licenses—a strange sort of trade! The custom-house officers mustered in crowds about the ship, ransacking every corner—barrels and bags, boxes and hampers of half-consumed provisions, empty bottles and full ones, musty straw and papers, and all that the dampness of a ship, pitch and tallow, and the human species confined in a narrow space, can produce of offensive sights and smells, were exposed to open day. These custom-house officers have seized a certain surplus of stores beyond what a ship is allowed to bring in port, whether the voyage has been long or short. I overheard the head seizer asking the Captain whether he preferred having his wine or his spirits seized; and the Captain seemed to take the proposal in very good part, and told me afterwards the man was very *friendly* to him. In this general confusion no breakfast could be expected; and permission being procured for the passengers to land, with their baggage, every one was eager to make his escape. I went on shore to reconnoitre, and to secure comfortable quarters, and brought back hot rolls—the olive-branch to the ark.

The houses, in a confused heap, crowd on the water; the tide washes their foundation; a black wall, built of rough stones, that stand on end, to facilitate the draining of the water, and steps, overgrown with sea-weeds, to ascend to the doors. Through one of these odd entrances I introduced my companions to the hotel —a strange, old, low building, extremely neat inside, with a tempting larder full in view, displaying, on shelves of tiles, fish of all sorts, fat fowls, &c. Well-dressed servants, civil and attentive, wait our commands. We are put in possession of a sitting-room and two bed-rooms. Our windows overlook two or three diminutive streets without foot-paths—too narrow, indeed, for any—all up and down, and crooked. It is Sunday. The men are, many of them, in volunteer uniforms, and look well enough for citizen-soldiers; the women highly dressed, or rather highly undressed, in extremely thin draperies, move about with an elastic gait on the light fantastic patten, making a universal clatter of iron on the pavement. Ruddy countenances, and *embonpoint,* are very general and striking. [Our] great astonishment was awakened at the sight of a sedan-chair, vibrating along on two poles. A monstrous carriage turned the corner of a street, overladed with passengers—a dozen, at least, on the top, before, and behind; all this resting on four high slender wheels, drawn along full speed on a rough unequal pavement. We observed some men, in old-fashioned cocked-hats with silver lace, compelling a Quaker to shut his shop *—which was opened again the moment they were gone. An elegant post-chaise and four stopped at the door. A young man, fat and fair, with the face and figure of a baby, six feet high, alighted from it; it was the first man of quality we had seen in England. He goes,

---

* By the Sunday Observance Act of 1677 shopkeepers were forbidden to trade on a Sunday. Fishmongers selling mackerel before and after divine service were exempted by a later Act of 1698; and an Act of 1794 allowed bakers to sell bread at certain hours. But no other tradesman could exercise any business "upon the Lords Day or any part thereof (workes of necessity and charity onely excepted)".

we are told, to lounge away his *ennui* and his idleness beyond seas —a premature attack of the *maladie du pays*. The English *maladie du pays* is of a peculiar character; it is not merely the result of extreme regrets when they have left their country, and of that perpetual longing to return, felt by other people, but an equal longing to leave it, and a sense of weariness and satiety all the time they are at home.

Dinner announced, suspended our observations; it was served in our own apartments. We had three small dishes, dressed very inartificially (an English cook only boils and roasts), otherwise very good. The table-linen and glass, and servants, remarkably neat, and in good order. At the dessert apples no bigger than walnuts, and without taste, which are said to be the best the country produces.

December 25.—I have been this morning to the custom house, with the other passengers, to get our passports. They obtained theirs without difficulty, but I must write to London for mine. Twenty-two years of absence have not expiated the original sin of being born in France: but I have no right to complain—an Englishman would be worse off in France.

We have on our arrival a double allowance of news; those which were coming over to us when we left America, and what has occurred since; an accumulation of about three months. The first thing we have learnt was an Imperial repudiation and an expected Imperial marriage, which seems to be a great stroke of policy.*

December 26.—I have been introduced to several respectable citizens of Falmouth; they all live in very small, old habitations, of which the apartments resemble the cabins of vessels. A new house is a phenomenon. The manners of this remote corner of England have retained a sort of primitive simplicity. I have seen nothing here of the luxury and pride which I expected to find everywhere in this warlike and commercial country. There is much despondency about Spain, and [all voices are raised] against the Walcheren expedition and against the ministers, who are not

* A few days before (on 16 December), Napoleon had divorced Josephine by an Act of Senate. He married Marie-Louise of Austria on 11 February the following year.

expected to withstand the shock of such general dissatisfaction.* We have left our hotel, to take furnished lodgings in an elevated part of the town—a kind of terrace—looking down upon the beautiful little harbour, and surrounding country. This apartment, composed of very small, neat rooms, costs only a guinea and a half a week, and the people of the house cook, and wait on us. This would cost more in the smallest town in America, or in fact could not be had. Domestics are here not only more obliging and industrious, but, what is remarkable, look better pleased and happier.

December 31.—We left Falmouth this morning, in a post-chaise, fairly on our way to London. The country is an extensive moor, covered with furze (a low thorny bush), evergreen, nipt by a few goats and sheep; not a fourth part of the surface is inclosed and cultivated. The total absence of wood is particularly striking to us, who have just arrived from a world of forests. It gives, however, a vastness to the prospect, and opens distances of great beauty; hills behind hills, clothed in brown and green, in an endless undulating line. The roads very narrow, crooked, and dirty; continually up and down. The horses we get are by no means good, and draw us with difficulty at the rate of five miles an hour. We change carriages as well as horses at every post-house; they are on four wheels, light and easy, and large enough for three persons. The post-boy sits on a cross bar of wood between the front springs, or rather rests against it. This is safer, and more convenient both for men and horses, but does not look well; and, as far as we have seen, English post-horses and postillions do not seem to deserve their reputation. This country (Cornwall), abounds in mines, which we have not time to visit. There is a singular sort of secondary mine, called *stream-tin*; the metal is found in very small particles, mixed in horizontal beds of clay.

---

* In Spain, Wellington had failed to advance after his victory at Talavera in July, and had been obliged to retreat on Portugal. The Walcheren Expedition —an invasion by 40,000 British troops of the Isle of Walcheren in the Scheldt with the object of capturing Antwerp and destroying the French fleet—had proved a disastrous failure.

January 1. 1810.—From Bodmin, where we slept last night, travelling all day, we have gone only 32 miles, through a very hilly, unpleasant country; a thick fog hid many a fine view from us. We have seen to-day several gentlemen's houses at a distance, spreading wide and low over fine lawns, with dark back-grounds of pines, and clumps of arbutus and laurel, as green as in spring. Near dusk, we crossed the bay to Plymouth Dock, amidst its floating castles, one of them bearing 90 guns. This place struck us as very like Philadelphia, and not the modern part of it. The inhabitants, however, do not look much like Quakers, being mostly army and navy.

January 4.—We slept last night at Exeter [having passed the previous night at Ivy Bridge, 'a pretty name and a pretty place, the inn superlatively comfortable'] and are arrived at Taunton; 64 miles in two days. We are in no haste. The approach of Exeter is very fine; you see from a hill the vast extent of country below, with an estuary at a distance, and hills in gentle swells lost in the horizon; it gives the idea of an ocean of cultivation. The cathedral is a venerable pile, built in the year 900, (my information comes from the old woman who showed it).*

The inside of the church is too light, I mean too *éclairé*, and the painted windows are not good. Those at one end were painted 400 years ago, my old woman said, and the other end within her remembrance; the one too early, probably, to be good, and the other too late. But when the service began, we forgot the church, and every thing else, in the beauty of the chant—angels in heaven cannot sing better! The organ, sweet, powerful, and solemn, formed a single accompaniment, without foppish flourishing.

The roads are full of soldiers, on foot and in carriages, travelling towards Plymouth—Portugal and India supposed to be their destination. The villages along the road are in general not beautiful—the houses very poor indeed; the walls old and rough, but the

---

* She was evidently an unreliable guide. Exeter Cathedral, a magnificent example of Decorated Gothic architecture, was, in fact, built between about 1275 and 1369, the west front between 1328 and 1375. It was completely restored under the direction of Sir George Gilbert Scott between 1870 and 1877.

windows generally whole and clean; no old hats or bundles of rags stuck in, as in America, where people build, but do not repair. Peeping in, as we pass along, the floors appear to be a pavement of round stones like the streets—a few seats, in the form of short benches—a table or two—a spinning-wheel—a few shelves—and just now (Christmas) greens hanging about. The people appear healthy, and not in rags, but not remarkably stout; the women, I think, are more so in proportion than the men. We meet very few beggars, and those old and infirm. Farm-houses, with their out buildings, look remarkably neat, and in great order; near them we see stacks of hay and straw, of prodigious size, covered with a slight thatching, and over that a sort of net of straw, to prevent the wind disturbing the thatch. Industry, method, and good order, are conspicuous everywhere. Most of the land is in meadow. Turnips are enormous; some as large as a man's head. The cattle do not look different from ours. We meet, however, with more *picturesque horses* than in America, with big shaggy legs, and heavy heads.

January 5.—Arrived in the evening at Bristol, 48 miles in eight hours, stoppages included; the horses better. On approaching Bristol, you see, from an elevation, a ridge on the left, covered with country-houses, groves of trees, and green fields. This ridge is intersected by a deep gap, near which a confused heap of roofs, towers, and steeples, and smoke, mark the town; dirty suburbs succeeded to this view; then a bridge over a mean and muddy stream; then through crowded streets we arrived at *The Bush.* The next morning shewed us, opposite our windows, a large building of freestone, in excellent style, *The Exchange.** Taking a guide, I called upon those for whom we had letters, and have been obligingly received. English hospitality is not in high repute —so far, we have no reason to complain of it. There is a look of comfort and neatness in the inside of houses, which is very striking; every thing is substantial and good, and uniformly so in all parts

---

* The architect of this much admired Exchange and Market (1741-3) was John Wood (1728-81) who, with his son, designed some of the best buildings in Bath.

of the house; and, as to the table, Lucullus dines with Lucullus every day, and little addition appears necessary should a few friends come unexpectedly. The creditable and decent look of the servants is no less remarkable, and they are the main-spring of all the other comforts. I am perfectly aware that there are many people who have no servants, and hardly bread to eat, and whose habitual state is labour and poverty. Although I have had no opportunity, as yet, of becoming acquainted with the situation of that class of people, I have necessarily seen them at their daily labour, in traversing the country, and I have had a glimpse of their habitations. All I can say is, that the poor do not look so poor here as in other countries; that poverty does not intrude on your sight; and that it is necessary to seek it. All human societies are full of it—here it does not overflow certainly. One of the best houses, and in the finest situation, (Clifton) costs L. 220 sterling a-year, taxes included—good houses, in an old-fashioned part of the town, are not one-fourth part of that rent. The wages of a man-servant, L. 35 sterling; a woman-cook, L. 15 sterling; meat sixpence and eightpence the pound.

January 8.—We arrived at Bath last night. The chaise drew up in style at the White Hart. Two well-dressed footmen were ready to help us to alight, presenting an arm on each side. Then a loud bell on the stairs, and lights carried before us to an elegantly furnished sitting-room, where the fire was already blazing. In a few minutes, a neat-looking chamber-maid, with an ample white apron, pinned behind, came to offer her services to the ladies, and shew the bed-rooms. In less than half an hour, five powdered *gentlemen* burst into the room with three dishes, &c. and two remained to wait. I give this as a sample of the best, or rather of the finest inns. Our bill was L. 2, 11s sterling, dinner for three, tea, beds, and breakfast. The servants have no wages—but, depending on the generosity of travellers, they find it their interest to please them. They (the servants) cost us about five shillings a-day.

This morning we have explored the town, which is certainly very beautiful. It is built of freestone, of a fine cream-colour, and contains several public edifices, in good taste. We remarked a circular place called the Crescent, another called the Circus—all the streets straight and regular. This town looks as if it had been cast in a mould all at once; so new, so fresh, and regular. The building where the medical water is drank, and where the baths are, exhibits very different objects; human nature, old infirm, and in ruins, or weary and *ennuyé*. Bath is a sort of great monastery, inhabited by single people, particularly superannuated females. No trade, no manufacturers, no occupations of any sort, except that of killing time, the most laborious of all. Half of the inhabitants do nothing, the other half supplies them with nothings:— Multitude of splendid shops, full of all that wealth and luxury can desire, arranged with all the arts of seduction.

Being in haste, and not equipped for the place, we left it at three o'clock, dined and slept 14 miles off, on the direct road to London. During our ride, we saw a little stream appear here and there among the willows, in the vale below. I asked a woman at the toll-gate what the name of it was: "Sure, Sir, the Avon!" It is not easy to avoid failing in respect to English rivers, by mistaking them for mere rivulets. I have heard an Englishman, who was amusing himself with the ignorance prevalent in foreign countries, tell a story of a lady, who said to him, "Have you in England any rivers like this?" (the Seine); but interrupting herself, added, laughingly, "Good God, how can I be so silly, it is an island; there are no rivers!" I really think the lady was not so very much in the wrong.

The country is beautiful, rich, and varied, with villas and mansions, and dark groves of pines—shrubs in full bloom, evergreen lawns, and gravel walks so neat—with porters' lodges, built in rough-cast, and stuck all over with flints, in their native grotesqueness; for this part of England is a great bed of chalk, full of this singular production (flints). They are broken to pieces with hammers, and spread over the road in deep beds, forming a hard and even surface, upon which the wheels of carriages make no impression. The roads are now wider; kept in good repair, and not deep, notwithstanding the season. The post-horses excellent; and post-boys riding instead of sitting. Our rate of travelling does not exceed six miles an hour, stoppages included; but we might go faster if we desired it. We meet with very few post-chaises, but a great many stage-coaches, mails, &c. and enormous broad wheel waggons. The comfort of the inns is our incessant theme at night —the pleasure of it is not yet worn out.

2

LONDON
11 January 1810 – 4 June 1810

January 11.—We arrived yesterday at Richmond. This morning I set out by myself for *town*, as London is called *par excellence,* in the stage-coach, crammed inside, and *herissé* outside with passengers, of all sexes, ages, and conditions. We stopped more than twenty times on the road—the debates about the fare of way-passengers—the settling themselves—the getting up, and the getting down, and damsels shewing their legs in the operation, and tearing and muddying their petticoats—complaining and swearing—took an immense time. I never saw any thing so ill managed. In about two hours we reached Hyde Park corner; I liked the appearance of it; but we were soon lost in a maze of busy, smoky, dirty streets, more and more so as we advanced. A sort of uniform dinginess seemed to pervade every thing, that is, the exterior; for through every door and window the interior of the house, the shops at least, which are most seen, presented, as we drove along, appearances and colours most opposite to this dinginess; everything there was clean, fresh, and brilliant. The elevated pavement on each side of the streets full of walkers, out of the reach of carriages, passing swiftly in two lines, without awkward interference, each taking to the left. At last a very indifferent street brought us in front of a magnificent temple, which I knew immediately to be St Paul's, and I left the vehicle to examine it. The effect was wonderfully beautiful; but it had less vastness than grace and magnificence. The colour struck me as strange—very black and very white, in patches which envelope sometimes half a column; the base of one, the capital of another—here, a whole row quite black—there, as white as chalk. It seemed as if there had been a fall of snow, and it adhered unequally.*

* This strange but not unpleasing contrast could be seen—and can still be seen—in other London buildings constructed of the same material, Portland Stone. The smoke blackened the walls; the rain washed those parts on which it freely fell.

I had not time for any long examination, and felt uneasy and helpless in the middle of an immense town, of which I did not know a single street. A hackney-coach seemed the readiest way to extricate myself, and I took one. After being dragged slowly along many short, winding, dark, and crowded streets, and missing my letters, which had just been sent to Richmond, I met with a friend, who took me under his protection; dismissed my hackney-coach, which was not better, and perhaps worse, than those of Paris, and in which I was surprised to find a litter of straw, which has a very shabby appearance, but, being changed every day, is better than a filthy carpet. My friend conducted me very obligingly back again through the whole town. In our walk we passed several large squares, planted in the middle with large trees and shrubs, over a smooth lawn, intersected with gravel walks; the whole inclosed by an iron railing, which protects these gardens against the populace, but does not intercept the view. The inhabitants of the neighbourhood, who contribute to the expence, have each a key. One of these squares, *Lincoln's Inn Fields*, appears to contain five or six acres, and is said to be equal to the base of the largest of the pyramids of Egypt. The buildings round are plain houses.* I have not observed any thing in this day's ramble above that rank in architecture, or any public building of note. But although the luxury of this people does not resemble the luxury of the Greeks and the Romans, yet they are better lodged. I have heard no cries in the streets—seen few beggars—no obstructions or stoppages of carriages—each taking to the left. We found in Piccadilly a stage-coach ready to start for Bath, by which I could be carried some miles on my way to Richmond; it resembled a ship on four wheels; a sort of half cylinder; round below, flat

---

* One house, at least, in Lincoln's Inn Fields was worthy of a more flattering description. This was Lindsey House, now Nos. 59–60. Built in 1640 when Inigo Jones, as Surveyor to the King, was responsible for the supervision of the development of the square, its design has been ascribed by Colen Campbell to the hand of the master himself. It was divided into two in 1751.

Sir John Soane's house, now the Soane Museum at 13–14, was not built until a few years after Simond's visit.

above, very long, and divided into three distinct apartments.* I was introduced into the cabin by an after-port, and locked in with another passenger. Soon after I had taken my seat, the carriage rattled away full speed. This was much better than my morning conveyance, and I enjoyed the change; but after a few miles, an apprehension seized me of being carried beyond the part to which I was bound (Kew Bridge). We reached it—I knew it again—saw with terror that we passed it, and that I was swept away with alarming velocity, like Robinson Crusoe from his island. I endeavoured in vain to call, or to open the door. At last the carriage stopped unexpectedly, little more than a quarter of a mile beyond the bridge; and, proceeding the rest of the way on foot, I reached Richmond long after dark, but in time for dinner, which is here an early supper—related the adventures of the day, and received the letters sent from London.

January 24.—We are at last established in London, in furnished lodgings, very near Portman Square, a fashionable part of the town.† A previous study of the map has made me sufficiently acquainted with the town to find my way to every part of it, by means of two principal avenues, Piccadilly and the Strand, Oxford Street and Holborn, which unite at St Paul's, whence, as from a common centre, they separate again, to form two other great avenues, still east and west, Cornhill and Bishopsgate Street: they are the arteries of this great body, and all the other streets are the veins, branching out in all directions. It is easier to acquire a practical knowledge of the geography of London than of Paris, which has not the same rallying points, except the Seine, which divides Paris more equally than the Thames does London; the other side of the Thames is only an extensive suburb, whereas the other side of the Seine is half Paris. The people of London, I find, are quite as disposed to answer obligingly to the questions of

* The stage-coaches for Richmond and the West Country left from the Bull and Mouth, 40 Piccadilly.

† Portman Square had been laid out but fifty years before. Its architectural masterpiece—and the main cause of its fashionable reputation—was the house on its northern side, No. 20, which had been finished in 1777, to the designs of Robert Adam, for the Countess of Home.

strangers as those of Paris. Whenever I have made inquiries, either in shops, or even from porters, carters, and market-women in the streets, I have uniformly received a civil answer, and every information in their power. People do not pull off their hats when thus addressing anybody, as would be indispensable at Paris; a slight inclination of the head, or motion of the hand, is thought sufficient. Foot-passengers walk on with ease and security along the smooth flag-stones of the side pavement. Their eyes, mine at least, are irresistibly attracted by the allurements of the shops, particularly print-shops; not that they always exhibit those specimens of the art so justly admired all over Europe, but oftener caricatures of all sorts. My countrymen, whenever introduced in them, never fail to be represented as diminutive, starved beings, of monkey-mien, strutting about in huge hats, narrow coats, and great sabres; an overgrown awkward Englishman crushes half a dozen of these pygmies at one squeeze. It must be owned, however, that the English do not spare themselves; their princes, their statesmen, and churchmen, are thus exhibited and hung up to ridicule, often with cleverness and humour, and a coarse sort of practical wit. Some shops exhibit instruments of mathematics, of optics, of chemistry, beautifully arranged; the admirable polish, and learned simplicity of the instruments, suggest the idea of justness and of perfection—recalling to your mind all you know of their uses, and inspiring a wish to know more. Jewellers' shops, glittering with costly trinkets, give me another sort of pleasure—that of feeling no sort of desire for any thing they contain. Finally, pastry-cook shops, which, about the middle of the day, and of the long interval between breakfast and dinner, are full of decent persons of both sexes, mostly men, taking a slight repast of tarts, buns, &c. with a glass of whey; it costs 6d. or 8d. sterling. A young and pretty woman generally presides behind the counter, as in the coffee-houses of Paris.

The inhabitants of London, such as they are seen in the streets, have, as well as the outside of their houses, a sort of a dingy, smoky look; not dirty absolutely—for you generally perceive clean linen —but the outside garments are of a dull, dark cast, and harmonize with mud and smoke. Prepossessed with a high opinion of English corpulency, I expected to see everywhere the original of *Jacques Roast-beef*. No such thing; the human race is here rather of mean stature—less so, perhaps, than the true Parisian race; but there is really no great difference; and I have met more than once with Sterne's little man, when, in turning round to help a child across the gutter, he saw with surprise a visage of fifty, where he expected to see one of five. The size of London draught-horses makes up for that of men; those which draw brewers' carts and coal-waggons are gigantic—perfect elephants! On the other hand, I have observed dwarf horses passing swiftly along the streets, mounted by boys, who appeared employed in carrying letters or messages. No armed watch, *guet*, or *marechaussée*, is ever met patroling the streets, or the highways; no appearance of police, and yet no apparent want of police; nothing disorderly.

February 17.—We have been a whole month in London, and for the last three weeks I have set down nothing in this journal. It is not, as might be supposed, from having been too much taken up, or too little. A French traveller once remarked sagaciously, that there is a malady peculiar to the climate of England, called the *catch-cold*; this malady, under the modern title of influenza, has recently afflicted all London, and we have been attacked by it. A friend of F. who had come to London on purpose to receive us, has been obliged to fly precipitately; others dare not come. The letters we brought have not procured many useful or agreeable acquaintances—some of them have not been followed by the slightest act of politeness; and although we have to acknowledge the attentions of some persons, their number is very small, and we feel alone in the crowd. London is a giant—strangers can only reach his feet. Shut up in our apartments, well warmed and well lighted, and where we seem to want nothing but a little of that immense society in the midst of which we are suspended, but not mixed, we have full leisure to observe its outward aspect and general movements, and listen to the roar of its waves, breaking around us in measured time, like the tides of the ocean.

In the morning all is calm—not a mouse stirring before ten o'clock; the shops then begin to open. Milk-women, with their pails perfectly neat, suspended at the two extremities of a yoke, carefully shaped to fit the shoulders, and surrounded with small tin measures of cream, ring at every door, with reiterated pulls, to hasten the maid-servants, who come half asleep to receive a measure as big as an egg, being the allowance of a family; for it is necessary to explain, that milk is not here either food or drink, but a tincture—an elixir exhibited in drops, five or six at most, in a cup of tea, morning and evening. It would be difficult to say what taste or what quality these drops may impart; but so it is; and nobody thinks of questioning the propriety of the custom. Not a single carriage—not a cart are seen passing. The first considerable stir is the drum and military music of the Guards, marching from their barracks to Hyde Park, having at their head three or four negro giants, striking, high, gracefully, and strong, the resounding cymbal. About three or four o'clock the fashionable world gives some signs of life, issuing forth to pay visits, or rather leave cards at the doors of friends, never seen but in the crowd of assemblies; to go to shops, see sights, or lounge in Bond Street—an ugly, inconvenient street, the attractions of which it is difficult to understand. At five or six they return home to dress for dinner. The streets are then lighted from one end to the other, or rather edged on either side with two long lines of little brightish dots, indicative of light, but yielding in fact very little—these are the lamps. They are not suspended in the middle of the streets as at Paris, but fixed on irons eight or nine feet high, ranged along the houses. The want of reflectors is probably the cause of their giving so little light. From six to eight the *noise* of wheels increases; it is the dinner hour. A multitude of carriages, with two eyes of flame staring in the dark before each of them, shake the pavement and the very houses, following and crossing each other at full speed. Stopping suddenly, a footman jumps down, runs to the door, and lifts the heavy knocker—gives a great knock—then several smaller ones in quick succession—then with all his might—flourishing as on a drum, with an art, and an air, and a delicacy of touch, which denote the quality, the rank, and the fortune of his master.

For two hours, or nearly, there is a pause; at ten a *redoublément* comes on. This is the great crisis of dress, of noise, and of rapidity—a universal hubbub; a sort of uniform grinding and shaking, like that experienced in a great mill with fifty pair of stones; and, if I was not afraid of appearing to exaggerate, I should say that it came upon the ear like the fall of Niagara, heard at two miles distance! This crisis continues undiminished till twelve or one o'clock; then less and less during the rest of the night—till, at the approach of day, a single carriage is heard now and then at a great distance.

Great assemblies are called routs or parties; but the people who give them, in their invitations only say, that they will be *at home* such a day, and this some weeks beforehand. The house in which this takes place is frequently stripped from top to bottom; beds, drawers, and all but ornamental furniture is carried out of sight, to make room for a crowd of well-dressed people, received at the door of the principal apartment by the mistress of the house standing, who smiles at every new comer with a look of acquaintance. Nobody sits; there is no conversation, no cards, no music; only elbowing, turning, and winding from room to room; then, at the end of a quarter of an hour, escaping to the hall door to wait for the carriage, spending more time upon the threshold among footmen than you had done above stairs with their masters. From this rout you drive to another, where, after waiting your turn to arrive at the door, perhaps, half an hour, the street being full of carriages, you alight, begin the same round, and end it in the same manner. The public knows there is a party in a house by two signs; first, an immense crowd of carriages before the house—then every curtain, and every shutter of every window wide open, shewing apartments all in a blaze of light, with heads innumerable, black and white (powdered or not), in continual motion. This custom is so general, that having, a few days ago, five or six persons in the evening with us, we observed our servant had left the windows thus exposed, thinking, no doubt, that this was a rout after our fashion.

Such may be, it will be said, the life of the rich, the well-born, and the idle, but it cannot be that of many of the people; of the commercial part, for instance, of this emporium of the trade of the universe. The trade of London is carried on in the east part of the town, called, *par excellence, the City.* The west is inhabited by people of fashion, or those who wish to appear such; and the line of demarcation, north and south, runs through Soho Square.* Every minute of longitude east is equal to as many degrees of gentility *minus*, or towards west, *plus*. This meridian line north and south, like that indicated by the compass, inclines west towards the north, and east towards the south, two or three points, in such a manner, as to place a certain part of Westminster on the side of fashion; the Parliament House, Downing Street, and the Treasury, are necessarily genteel. To have a right to emigrate from east to west, it is requisite to have at least L. 3000 sterling a-year; should you have less, or at least spend less, you might find yourself slighted; and L. 6000 a-year would be safer. Many, indeed, have a much narrower income, who were born there; but city emigrants have not the same privileges.

One thing surprises me more and more every day; it is the great number of people in the opposition; that is, those who disapprove, not only the present measures of ministers, which have not been of late either very wise or very successful, but the form and constitution of the government itself. It is stigmatized as vicious, corrupt, and in its decay, without hope or remedy but in a general reform, and in fact a revolution. Our acquaintance, though not very extensive, is sufficiently various to afford a fair sample of public opinion. I have had an idea of making a list in three columns, whigs, tories, and absolute reformers—and it would not be difficult; for there are a few principal topics, which, like cabalistic words, it is enough to touch upon, to know at once the whole train of opinions of those with whom you speak. It appears to me that the tories, or friends of the administration, and of all administrations, are in a small minority; of the two other parties, one does not seem disposed to approve of any administration, and neither of them of the present; and, supposing the ministerial power to rest on public opinion, one might be tempted to exclaim

* Regent Street, already planned at this time though not yet begun, was conceived not merely as a grand route between the Prince's palatial Carlton House and the royal Marylebone Park, but also as a convenient swathe between the two sides of London which Simond, like all visitors, noted as being so contrasting: the new, expensive developments to the west and the poorer districts around Soho to the east.

with Basil in the Barbier de Seville, "*Qui est ce donc que l'on trompe—tout le mond est du secret?*" This is a most alarming state of things—a spark might set the whole political machine in a blaze; and yet, looking around at the appearance of all things, it seems a pity that so much good should necessarily be abandoned in pursuit of better, and by the means of a revolution. Every body disclaims a revolution *à la Française*; but who is so presumptuous as to fancy a revolution, when once begun, can be guided and stopped at pleasure? Notwithstanding their lamentations and complaints, and the avowed expectation of a dreadful crisis, the inhabitants of London live just as if they had nothing to fear; amuse themselves, and attend to their business in perfect security. It would seem as if all this clamour was only habit, a sort of plaintive mania—and yet they appear so much in earnest that I do not know what to think of it.*

March 5.—It is difficult to form an idea of the kind of winter days in London; the smoke of fossil coals forms an atmosphere, perceivable for many miles, like a great round cloud attached to the earth. In the town itself, when the weather is cloudy and foggy, which is frequently the case in winter, this smoke increases the general dingy hue, and terminates the length of every street with a fixed grey mist, receding as you advance. But when some rays of sun happens to fall on this artificial atmosphere, its impure mass assumes immediately a pale orange tint, similar to the effect of Claude Lorraine glasses—a mild golden hue, quite beautiful. The air, in the mean time, is loaded with small flakes of smoke, in sublimation—a sort of flower of soot, so light as to float without falling. This black snow sticks to your clothes and linen, or lights on your face. You just feel something on your nose, or your cheek

---

* This view of public opinion in London in February 1810 is fully corroborated by other observers. The well-to-do angrily complained of a ruinous income tax of 10% which had been imposed on all incomes over £200 in 1798 and which was to continue until the end of the war; the middle-class merchant was exasperated by the sudden closing down of markets which the war entailed and by the wild rise and fall of prices; many of the working-class were close to starvation and felt compelled to conclude that the Government—which had made Trade Unions illegal by the Combination Acts—were as much concerned in keeping them in subjection as in defeating Napoleon.

—the finger is applied mechanically, and fixes it into a black patch!

An English dinner is very different from a French one; less so, however, than formerly—the art of cookery being in fact now half French. England was always under great obligations to its neighbours in that respect; and most of the culinary terms are French, as well as those of tactics. It is singular, that the same animal which, when living, has an English name, has a French one when slaughtered. A sheep becomes mutton; an ox, beef; and a hog, pork. I overheard, the other day, an old Frenchman, who has lived thirty years among the English, tell one of his children who happened to have dirty hands, to go and wash them, adding, by way of reproof, "Go, you are a little *pork*." Such misapplications of words shock like discords in music, or ill-assorted colours, the more as they come nearer without being right, and are extremely ludicrous.

The master and mistress of the house sit at each end of the table —narrower and longer than the French tables—the mistress at the upper end—and the places near her are the places of honour. There are commonly two courses and a dessert. I shall venture to give a sketch of a moderate dinner for ten or twelve persons. Although contemporary readers may laugh, I flatter myself it may prove interesting in future ages.

FIRST COURSE.

Oyster Sauce.	Fowls.	Vegetables.
Fish.	Soup.	Roasted or Boiled Beef.
Spinage.	Bacon.	Vegetables.

SECOND COURSE.

Creams.	Pastry.	Cauliflowers.
Ragôut à la Françoise.	Cream.	Game.
Celery.	Macaroni.	Pastry.

DESSERT.

Walnuts.		Raisins and Almonds.
Apples.	Cakes.	Pears.
Raisins and Almonds.		Oranges.

London

Soon after dinner the ladies retire, the mistress of the house rising first, while the men remain standing. Left alone, they resume their seats, evidently more at ease, and the conversation takes a different turn—less reserved—and either graver, or more licentious:

> Le dîner fait, on digère, on raisonne,
> On conte, on rit, on médit du prochain.

Politics are a subject of such general interest in England, both for men and women, that it engrosses the conversation before, as much as after the retreat of the ladies; the latter, indeed, are still more violent and extravagant than the men, whenever they meddle at all with politics, and the men out of Parliament, I think, more than those in Parliament. Women, however, do not speak much in numerous and mixed company. Towards the end of dinner, and before the ladies retire, bowls of coloured glass full of water are placed before each person. All (women as well as men) stoop over it, sucking up some of the water, and returning it, often more than once, and, with a spitting and washing sort of noise, quite charming—the operation frequently assisted by a finger elegantly thrust into the mouth! This done, and the hands dipped also, the napkins, and sometimes the table-cloth, are used to wipe hand and mouth. This, however, is nothing to what I am going to relate. Drinking much and long leads to unavoidable consequences. Will it be credited, that, in a corner of the very dining-room, there is a certain convenient piece of furniture, to be used by any body who wants it. The operation is performed very deliberately and undisguisedly, as a matter of course, and occasions no interruption of the conversation. I once took the liberty to ask why this convenient article was not placed out of the room, in some adjoining closet; and was answered, that, in former times, when good fellowship was more strictly enforced than in these degenerate days, it had been found that men of weak heads or stomachs took advantage of the opportunity to make their escape shamefully, before they were quite drunk; and that it was to guard against such an enormity, that this nice expedient had been invented. I have seen the article in question regularly provided in houses where there was no man, that is, no master of the house; the mistress, therefore, must be understood to have given the necessary orders to her servants—a supposition rather alarming for the delicacy of an English lady. Yet I find these very people up in arms against some uncleanly practices of the French; for instance, spitting on the floor, the carpet, &c. &c. or spreading in full view a snuff-taking handkerchief, with an innocence of nastiness quite inconceivable. To take a lump of sugar with their fingers, is another offence the French are apt to give, but of a lesser dye. Dr Johnson was once exposed to an abomination of the latter sort during his tour in France, and the astonishment and wrath of the Doctor are faithfully recorded somewhere.*

It may be a matter of curiosity in France to know how the people of London are lodged. Each family occupy a whole house, unless very poor. There are advantages and disadvantages attending this custom. Among the first, the being more independent of the noise, the dirt, the contagious disorders, or the danger of your neighbour's fires, and having a more complete home. On the other hand, an apartment all on one floor, even of a few rooms only, looks much better, and is more convenient. These narrow houses, three or four stories high—one for eating, one for sleeping, a third for company, a fourth under ground for the kitchen, a fifth perhaps at top for the servants—and the agility, the ease, the quickness with which the individuals of the family run up and down, and perch on the different stories, give the idea of a cage with its sticks and birds. The plan of these houses is very simple, two rooms on each story; one in the front with two or three windows looking on the street, the other on a yard behind, often very small; the stairs generally taken out of the breadth of the backroom. The ground-floor is usually elevated a few feet above the

* The abomination is recorded in Boswell's *Life of Johnson*, first published in 1791: "'The French are an indelicate people; they will spit upon any place. At Madame ——'s, a literary lady of rank, the footman took the sugar in his fingers, and threw it into my coffee. I was going to put it aside; but hearing it was made on purpose for me, I e'en tasted Tom's fingers. The same lady would needs make tea *à l'Angloise*. The spout of the tea pot did not pour freely; she bade the footman blow into it. France is worse than Scotland in everything but climate.'"

level of the street, and separated from it by an area, a sort of ditch, a few feet wide, generally from three to eight, and six or eight feet deep, inclosed by an iron railing; the windows of the kitchen are in this area. A bridge of stone or brick leads to the door of the house. The front of these houses is about twenty or twenty-five feet wide; they certainly have rather a paltry appearance—but you cannot pass the threshold without being struck with the look of order and neatness of the interior. Instead of the abominable filth of the common entrance and common stairs of a French house, here you step from the very street on a neat floor-cloth or carpet, the wall painted or papered, a lamp in its glass bell hanging from the ceiling, and every apartment in the same style—all is neat, compact, and independent, or, as it is best expressed here, snug and comfortable—a familiar expression, rather vulgar perhaps, from the thing itself being too common.

The streets have all common sewers, which drain the filth of every house. The drains preclude that awkward process by which necessaries are emptied at Paris, poisoning the air of whole streets, during the night, with effluvia, hurtful and sometimes fatal to the inhabitants. Rich houses have what are called water-closets; a cistern in the upper story, filled with rain-water, communicates by a pipe and cock to a vessel of earthenware, which it constantly washes. The rent of a house of the class described, which is of the middling or low kind, varies in different parts of the town, from L. 80 to L. 200 Sterling, including the taxes, which are from L. 20 to L. 50. The following sketch will give you an idea of one of the best houses, This is the first story. Below, on the ground-floor, the front room, 24 feet by 30, is the eating-room; the one 18 by 22 is the servants' hall. This house was bought by the present proprietor for L. 16,000 sterling, but had cost nearly double in building. The rent of houses a little inferior is L. 400 or L. 500 sterling a-year, including taxes; but there are houses the rent of which is L. 1000 a-year. The best houses are occupied by the proprietors themselves. The establishment of such a house as is described above, is from four to six male servants, and probably as many women—the wages of the former, L. 40 sterling, dress included; and of the latter, L. 10 to L. 12; and the whole annual expence, L. 4000 to L. 6000 sterling. Butcher meat is as follows: Beef and mutton, 8d.; veal, 1s. to 1s. 6d.; butter, 1s. 10d.; bread, 3d. the pound; a good cow, L. 18 to L. 20 sterling; a good horse, L. 50 to L. 100 sterling.

March 30.—I had long intended to go to the House of Commons, but wished to get some person used to the place to go with me. I found, however, that few people liked to encounter the trouble, and fatigue, and, I might almost say, the humiliations to which an admission to the gallery exposes you, whenever the business before the House is at all interesting, therefore I took my determination, and went alone yesterday.* The door of the gallery opened at four. A great crowd, accumulated on the stairs two hours before, pressed in at once through a narrow door, where your title of admission is demanded; mine was an order from a member; but I observed that a five shilling piece was the most usual passport, received openly, and more graciously than my legitimate order. I found, on entering, the first and second rows full, sat on the third, and had two more rows of benches behind me. The house below was thin of members; they were employed in some minor business. A tall, slender, and genteel-looking man rose to give notice of a motion he intended to make next week, respecting an act of oppression and cruelty of a captain of a ship of war against one of his sailors. He said only a few words: — This was Sir Francis Burdett, a very notorious gentleman at present.† The Walcheren business was then taken up—General T.

---

* The Houses of Parliament then met in a conglomeration of buildings of all styles and periods which had been put up around Westminster Hall. There are good illustrations of them in Partington's *Views of London* which was published in 1834 the year of their total destruction by fire.

† Sir Francis Burdett (1770–1844), a passionate advocate of popular rights, was a determined Radical opponent of Pitt and the war with France. According to Cobbett he was the most influential and popular man in England with the "really efficient part of the people". He was considered particularly "notorious" at this time because of his support of a fellow Radical, John Gale Jones, who had been committed to prison by the House of Commons. He published a version of his speech defending Jones in Cobbett's *Weekly Register* with consequences which Simond later relates.

spoke against the ministers;* General C. and Mr R. for them; all at great length, and, as it appeared to me, very heavily. Then several young members came forward, that is to say, spoke, which is done without leaving their places, and merely standing up; Lord P. Lord G. G. and Mr F.—this last member spoke with great vehemence in favour of ministers—all three with a sort of school-boy oratory, well enough as a lesson for practice, but to no sort of purpose as to persuading or changing any opinion. A veteran member arose next, old and toothless, and speaking like a Jew, uncouthly and carelessly, but ardently, and with that seeming self-conviction, which is among the very first requisites for eloquence. He stepped forward on the floor towards the table, and used animated gestures, a little *à la Française*, or at least very different from the English mode of oratory. Mr Grattan is Irish. All this lasted till eleven. I felt quite weary; my legs cramped from sitting so long, for you are forbidden to stand up for a moment; and, giving up the point, I went home....

I have been carried to one of the hospitals of this great town, supported by voluntary contributions. I shall relate what I saw. The physician, seated at a table in a large hall on the ground-floor, with a register before him, ordered the door to be opened; a crowd of miserable objects, women, pushed in, and ranged themselves along the wall; he looked in his book, and called them to him successively. Such a one! The poor wretch, leaving her wall, crawled to the table. "How is your catarrh?" "Please your honour, no offence I hope, it is the asthma. I have no rest night nor day, and"—"Ah, so it is an asthma! It is somebody else who has the catarrh. Well, you have been ordered to take, &c."—"Yes, Sir, but I grow worse and worse, and—"—"That is nothing, you must go on with it."—"But, Sir, indeed I cannot."—"Enough, enough,

---

* Sir Banastre Tarleton (1754–1833), M.P. for Liverpool. He had served under Clinton and Cornwallis in America. The other Members to whom the author refers are Sir Charles Gregan-Craufurd, brother of Robert Craufurd the famous commander of the Light Division in the Peninsula; George Rose, M.P. for Christchurch; Lord Porchester; Lord George Grenville; William Fitzgerald; and Henry Grattan, then aged sixty-five and one of the Irish members for Dublin.

good woman, I cannot listen to you any more; many patients to get through this morning—never do to hear them talk—go and take your draught, &c."—The catarrh woman made way for a long train of victims of consumption, cases of fever, dropsy, scrofula, and some disorders peculiar to women, detailed, without any ceremony, before young students. This melancholy review of human infirmities, was suddenly interrupted by the unexpected entrance of a surgeon, followed by several young men, carrying a piece of bloody flesh on a dish. "A curious case," they exclaimed, placing the dish on the table; "an ossification of the lungs! Such a one, who died yesterday—just opened. This is the state of his lungs. See these white needles, like fish-bones, shooting through here and there—most curious indeed." Then they handled, and cut open, and held up between the eye and the light, these almost palpitating remains of a creature who breathed yesterday! The symptoms of his disorder, and the circumstances of his death, were freely talked over, and accurately described in the hearing of consumptive patients, who felt, I dare say, the bony needles pricking their own lungs at every breath they drew, and seemed to hear their own sentence of death pronounced.

The women being dispatched, twenty or thirty male spectres came in, and underwent the same sort of summary examination. The only case I recollect was that of a man attacked with violent palpitations, accompanied with great pain in the shoulder. His heart was felt beating hard through the sternum, or even under the ribs on the *right* side. His heart has moved from its place!— The unhappy man, thrown back on an arm-chair—his breast uncovered—pale as death—fixed his fearful eyes on the physicians, who successively came to feel the pulsations of that breast, and reason on the cause. They seemed to me to agree among themselves, that the heart had been pushed on one side by the augmentation of bulk of the viscera; and that the action of the aorta was impeded thereby. The case excited much attention—but no great appearance of compassion. They reasoned long on the cause, without adverting to the remedy till after the patient had departed— when he was called back from the door, and cupping prescribed!

April 4.—Some military men whom we saw lately spoke unfavourably of Congreve's rockets. They are made like common rockets, only of an enormous size. The cylinder, or case of iron, contains 20 or 30 pounds of powder, rammed hard, and the forepart loaded with balls. The rocket is impelled by its own recoil. It is held, in the first instance, by a pole 20 or 25 feet long, sloping to the proper angle like a mortar. The pole is carried away by the rocket, and keeps it in its proper direction like the feather of an arrow. But when the wind blows strong with it, or sidewise, the pole or tail is apt to steer the wrong course; and the rockets go right only against the wind, or with no wind. At Flushing, they steered back again upon the British troops, and did *more harm than good*. At Copenhagen they succeeded perfectly, and then, of course, did *more good than harm*. They have been used sometimes in Spain with great effect. As a proof of their doubtful utility, these officers remarked that Bonaparte had not as yet adopted them.*

April 10.—London has been in the greatest ferment for the last four days, in consequence of the vote passed the 5th instant by the House of Commons, for the imprisonment in the Tower of Sir Francis Burdett, one of their own members, for a libel against that House published by him, which is an offence against their privileges. From the morning of the 6th to the morning of the 9th, the sergeant-at-arms, with the order of the House in his hand, and an army of 40,000 or 50,000 men at his heels, hesitated whether he should force open the door of Sir Francis, who sets at defiance the order of his colleagues, and maintains they have no right to invade his house.

---

* There was much prejudice in the Army against these rockets, the invention of the ingenious William Congreve (1772–1828), whose talents were much admired by the Prince Regent. Wellington shared the prejudice. "I don't want to set fire to any town," he wrote home from the Peninsula, "and I don't know any other use of rockets." Lieutenant-Colonel Sir Augustus Frazer of the Royal Horse Artillery—although he too was disappointed with their general performance at first—refused to abandon them, however, until they had been thoroughly tested. And at the crossing of the Adour in February 1814, these "formidable spitfires" deafeningly noisy and accurately aimed, proved so extraordinarily effective that, in the words of a German observer, "the enemy at once retreated in great confusion".

During this interval, the populace, always bold against timidity and indecision, took part for Sir Francis; and, mustering in great force before his house, sent showers of brick-bats upon those passengers, either on foot or in carriages, who neglected to conform to certain patriotic demonstrations. At night they proceeded to the houses of the members whom they supposed inimical to Sir Francis, breaking their windows, and occasionally those of their neighbours; and in the ardour of their zeal, mistaking friends for foes, they broke the windows, and even the stone steps of some members in the opposition. Sir John [Anstruther] was one of them. The Life Guards were grossly insulted; wounded with stones thrown at them, and by frequent falls of their horses on the smooth pavement. At last the serjeant-at-arms and his assistant, penetrating into the house, partly by force and partly by address, secured their prisoner, and carried him to the Tower in a carriage, escorted by a strong detachment. This detachment was, on its return, saluted with frequent volleys of brick-bats, till at last they were provoked to fire, and a number of individuals were killed and wounded, most of whom were unfortunately innocent spectators.

Mr Cobbett in his Political Register of yesterday, would have us believe that the people were unanimous for Sir Francis—but it appeared to me far otherwise.* I was much on the spot, and observed more curiosity than earnestness or interest among the crowd; and I think it very probable that the brick-bat men were not many, and that the same individuals acted successively at the different scenes of action.

April 18.—There was yesterday a meeting of the electors of Westminster, legally convened for the purpose of petitioning Parliament for the liberation of their representative, Sir Francis Burdett, and new disorders were apprehended. The language of the petition is certainly violent, and in fact a mere vehicle for rude

* William Cobbett (1763–1855), the son of a Surrey farmer, emigrated in 1793 to the United States where he published a daily newspaper, *Porcupine's Gazette*. On his return to England in 1800, he became a reformer. His *Weekly Register* was started in 1802. For his consistent attacks upon flogging in the Army—a campaign supported and encouraged by Sir Francis Burdett, from whom he received a good deal of financial support—Cobbett was fined £1,000 and imprisoned for two years in 1810.

censure, and abuse of the House of Commons; but the meeting was peaceable, and all this will end in a war of words.

There is now light and length of day sufficient to see the sights of this capital. We have begun by the British Museum. The building is disposed round a vast court, and in very good taste. You are to wait in the hall of entrance till fourteen other visitors are assembled, for the rule is, that fifteen persons are to be admitted at one time, neither more nor less. This number completed, a German ciceroni took charge of us, and led us *au pas de charge* through a number of rooms full of stuffed birds and animals—many of them seemingly in a state of decay. We had a glimpse of arms, dresses, and ornaments of savages hung around—of a collection of minerals—next of antiquities from Herculaneum and Pompeia, and monstrous Egypt. We remarked a treble inscription on a large block of dark porphyry, brought from Rosetta; one is in hieroglyphics, one in the common language of Egypt, and one in Greek—all three saying the same thing serve as a glossary to each other. This stone, and several large sarcophagi, and numerous statues, and basso-relievos, belonged to the French collection which fell into the hands of the British in 1801. The last and most valuable acquisitions are the Greek and Roman marbles brought from Italy by Mr Townly.* We had just time to notice a very fine statue of Diana, and a bust of a woman looking up with a great expression of indignation and terror; the more remarkable, from the general calmness and tranquillity of antiques. The merit, however, of a considerable part of these marbles, consists mostly of their being undoubtedly antique. Among the manuscripts, we observed in the catalogue 43 volumes of Icelandic literature, presented by Sir Joseph Banks, who visited that singular island 40 years ago—41 volumes of decisions of the commisaries who settled the boundaries of properties after the great fire of London, which destroyed 400 streets and 13000 houses, says Hume, in 1666. The damage was estimated, at the time, at L.10,716,000 sterling, equal to L. 28,000,000 sterling now. 'The city was left a vast plain of

* Charles Towneley (1737–1805) had begun his collection of marbles and terracotta during a residence in Italy in 1768. It was purchased from his executors by the British Museum.

rubbish. We noticed also an original deed of some land to a monastery, dated Ravenna, Anno Dom.572, written on the papyrus; and the original of Magna Charta. We had no time allowed to examine any thing; our conductor pushed on without minding questions, or unable to answer them, but treating the company with double *entendres* and witticisms on various subjects of natural history, in a style of vulgarity and impudence which I should not have expected to have met in this place, and in this country.*

We have just seen Madame Catalini†—she is a bewitching creature, and, notwithstanding our high expectations, she has exceeded them. Her voice, which is strong, clear, and harmonious, and produced without effort or contorsions, is the least of her attractions. The grace and the modesty of her appearance—the *naïveté*—the archness of her smile, tender and playful at the same time, charmed us still more than her voice. Des Hayes and Vestris are winged Mercuries,‡ this Vestris is, however, said to be in-

---

* At this time the heterogeneous collections of the British Museum were crowded into the rooms of Montague House in Great Russell Street, the former residence of the Dukes of Montagu. It was not until the 1820's that the present Museum was built around it, to the designs of Robert Smirke; not until the 1850's that its "vast court" was built over to make the huge domed Reading Room; not until the 1880's that all the natural history exhibits—the stuffed birds and animals, past which Simond was hurried by the guide—were removed to the new specialist museum in South Kensington.

Simond's strictures were well deserved. Before 1810 the Museum's exhibits were shown only to gentlemen who could obtain a ticket; and after 1810 although they were shown three days a week to "any person of decent appearance who may apply", visitors were admitted grudgingly. Some reforms were carried out by Joseph Planta, Principal Librarian from 1799 to 1827; but not before Antonio Panizzi brought his great gifts to bear on the Museum's reconstruction did it achieve a worthy reputation.

† Angelica Catalini (1779–1849), the Italian singer, had made her debut in Venice in 1797. She appeared several times at Covent Garden.

‡ Andre-Jean Deshayes (1777–1864), the son of the *maître de ballet* of the Comédie-Française, was the *premier danseur* of the Opéra.

Armand Vestris (1787–1825) was the first husband of Lucia Elizabeth Vestris, née Bartolozzi, the actress who later married Charles James Mathews, afterwards manager of Covent Garden. The performance described took place at the King's Theatre on 3 May and was a benefit night for Madame Catalini.

ferior to the others. Some of my countrymen have assured me, in confidence, that he would not be endured in Paris—it may be so—I have not had the honour of being lately at Paris. The Opera-house of London is, like all the theatres I have seen in England, in the shape of a horse-shoe.* The side-boxes are ill turned to see, and the front ones too far to hear. The height of the ceiling is so great that the voice is lost. It seems strange that the semicircular shape should not have occurred, or should not have been adopted. Each spectator would have the actors precisely in front of him, and at a mean distance equal for all. Such a theatre would moreover contain more spectators. I would lower the ceiling one-third at least, dispensing with the two upper tiers of boxes. It would be a very small pecuniary sacrifice—this high region being always but thinly filled, and by spectators whose presence, or behaviour at least, is either a great scandal, or very inconvenient—that is to say, in the side-galleries, certain ladies, who carry on their business quite openly, selling and delivering the articles they trade in under the eye of the public, and with a degree of shamefulness for which the inhabitants of Otaheite alone can furnish any precedent. That part of the upper region which fronts the stage is occupied by a less indecent, but more noisy sort of people; sailors, footmen, low tradesmen and their wives and mistresses, who enjoy themselves, drinking, whistling, howling as much as they please. These gods, for so they are called from their elevated station, which is in France denominated the *paradis*, assume the high prerogative of hurling down their thunder on both actors and spectators, in the shape of nut-shells, cores of apples, and orange-peel. This innocent amusement has always been considered in

* The original Covent Garden Theatre had been burned down two years before. The new one—designed by Robert Smirke—had only just been completed. The horse-shoe shape, which Simond condemns, had been introduced into England by the Polish architect, Michael Novosielsky—who rebuilt Vanbrugh's opera house in the Haymarket in 1789—and had since become the standard shape for London theatres, though the theatre at Bristol, finished in 1766, had demonstrated the advantages of the semi-circular end favoured in France. In 1856 Smirke's theatre, like its predecessor, was destroyed by fire. The present building on the site was built between 1856 and 1858 by Edward M. Barry.

England as a sort of exuberance of liberty, of which it is well to have a little too much, to be sure that you have enough. Going to the play is not a habit with anybody here; it is in fact unfashionable: but London is so large, and the theatres so few, that they are always full. Paris has twenty-three theatres; London four or five, and these shut up part of the year. The hour of dining is precisely that of the play, which is another considerable obstacle.*

Mrs Siddons has at last made her appearance, yesterday (the 25th April) in the Grecian Daughter. She appears about fifty—her voice is a little broken—and F— was at first disagreeably affected at the change twenty years had produced.† With fewer natural advantages, her talents remain the same, and she is certainly a very great actress. The house was quite full. Her younger brother, C. Kemble, acted; he has very dramatic features, and a great command of countenance.‡

April 29—We have seen Mrs Siddons again in the Gamester, and she was much greater than on the first day. Perfect simplicity, deep sensibility, her despair in the last scene, mute and calm, had a prodigious effect. There was not a dry eye in the house—the most profound silence pervaded an assembly of people of all sorts, in the gallery as well as everywhere else. Mrs Siddons had touched a chord which vibrates in all hearts. We were placed farther from the stage than the first day, (in the pit, unmindful of consequences) and Mrs Siddons appeared still young and handsome. Cooke played Stukely *con amore*. He is an excellent actor, who delights (a strange taste) in these parts of scoundrels.** This one (Stukely) is an amateur of baseness—he glories in it, and boasts of

---

* The other main London theatres in 1810, apart from Covent Garden and the Theatre Royal, Haymarket (rebuilt by John Nash in 1820-1), were Drury Lane (rebuilt after a fire by Benjamin Wyatt in 1809), and the Lyceum (rebuilt by Samuel Beazley in 1816 and again in 1831—only the portico now survives).

† Sarah Siddons (1755-1831) was, in fact, fifty-five. She formally retired from the stage two years later.

‡ Charles Kemble (1775-1854) was one of three of Mrs Siddons's brothers who achieved fame as an actor. He was the father of Fanny Kemble.

** George Frederick Cooke (1756-1811) was, in Edmund Kean's opinion, the greatest actor on the London stage. He died in New York the year after this performance in *The Gamester*.

it, which is not in nature. There is still a sort of modesty in vice which shrinks from a naked exhibition, and dreads even to see the secret image reflected from its own bosom.

April 20—A new panorama is now exhibiting in London; it is of Flushing. The spectator is placed in the middle of the town, on the top of some high building: bombs and rockets pierce the roofs of the houses, which are instantly in flames, or burst in the middle of the streets, full of the dismayed inhabitants, flying from their burning dwellings with their effects, and carrying away the sick and wounded. It is a most terrifying picture. At the sight of so much misery, all the common-places about war become again original, and the sentimental lamentations on suffering humanity oppress and sicken the soul, as if they were uttered for the first time.*

The English are great in practical mechanics. In no country in the world are there, perhaps, so many happy applications of that science, I might say, of that peculiar sense, of that instinct of the human species. A gentleman of the name of Mann has invented a wooden-leg of ingenious construction; an elastic spring wraps round the heel, continues under the sole of the foot, to the extremity of the toes, in such a manner as to imitate exactly the double motion of these parts in walking. There are of course joints. The artificial limb is made on the model of the natural one; it is hollow; the stump hangs in it, but is stopped at the knee, which rests in a sort of funnel, so exactly adapted, that the junction does not appear, and that the part is enabled to bear, without any inconvenience, the weight of the body in walking. I heard, with surprise, of a gentleman of our acquaintance having one of these wooden-legs, without my having observed it; and a young lady in the same situation is so slightly lame, that it is impossible to say on which side it is. Mr Mann was first led to turn his mind to this subject, from a desire to relieve his own brother, who had lost his leg above the knee; and his fraternal affection has, in the end, made his fortune.

* Flushing had been bombarded for two nights and days during the calamitous Walcheren expedition in 1809. Half the town was burned, and six hundred civilians were killed.

Pugilism is a regular science in England, as fencing is in France. Fighting for improvement is called sparring—and in good earnest, boxing. In sparring, the hand is covered with much the same sort of glove as in fencing. I have been taken to a fives-court, where I have seen some of the best professors, and some amateurs of this noble art, spar. Two combatants, naked to the waist, ascended a theatre or stage, fifteen or twenty feet square, and three or four feet high, erected in the centre of the five's-court; each had his second; they shook hands, like the salute in fencing—then on their guard; one foot forward—knees a little bent—the principal weight of the body on the foremost leg—fist held to the height of the chin, at the distance of about a foot. In this attitude the combatants observe each other, eye to eye, watching their opportunity to place a blow, which is darted, rather than struck, with the back of the hand or knuckles; a moderate blow, well planted, gives a fall. The blows are parried with the outside of the arm, or with one hand, while the other returns the blow. The pugilists are very sparing of their strength and their wind; no unnecessary motion— no precipitation—and, above all, no anger. One of the first requisites is impassibility under the severest bodily pain. Notwithstanding the gloves, blood is spilt sometimes. Among the performers at the fives-court, Crib the younger, Gulley, and Belcher, were pointed out to me—all names of renown in the art.* They were not stout men, but remarkable for activity and coolness. The place was very full—a mixed company of people of all ranks—a considerable proportion of men of fashion; and all went off in a very orderly and quiet manner. The sword or pistol equalize strength, and secure politeness and circumspection between individuals in the higher ranks of society; the fist answers the same purpose between the high and the low. A gentleman well taught can by that means repress and punish vulgar insult, when supported by mere

---

* Tom Cribb (1781–1848), a former coal-porter known as the Black Diamond, had won his first public fight five years before after seventy-six rounds. He twice defeated Jem Belcher who was English champion in the early 1790's, and had himself been champion for nearly ten years when he retired in 1821. John Gully (1783—1863), the third prize-fighter whom Simond saw, became M.P. for Pontefract and the father of twenty-four children.

The rural scene: drilling and harrowing

Bristol Cathedral and college green

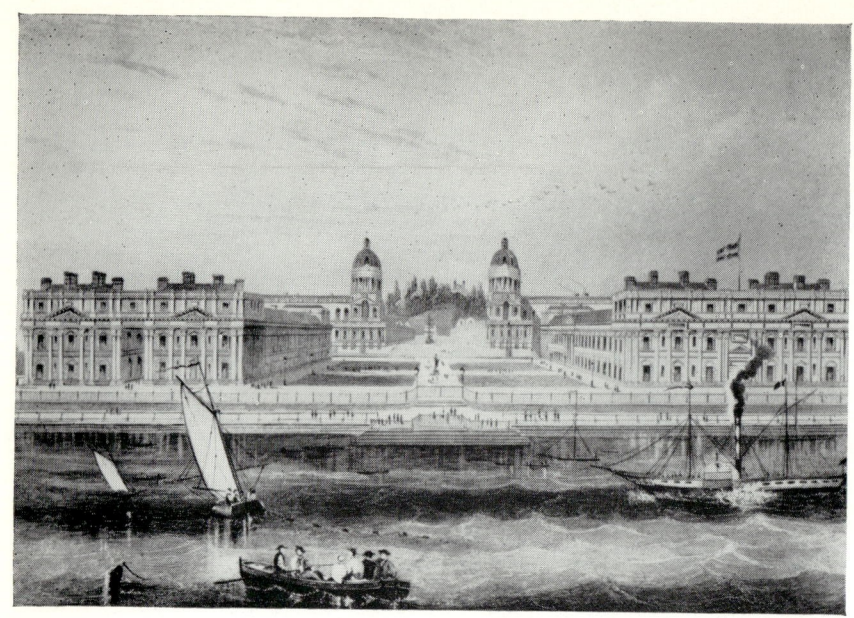

Façade for surgery: Greenwich Hospital

Chester: Lower Bridge Street

John Barrister: 'an excellent English actor' (1760–1836)

Panoply of death: a soldier's funeral

bodily strength. There is a sort of courtesy and law of combat here, as well as in more deadly encounters. You are not to strike an enemy on the ground, and never below the waist; you are to desist the instant he gives out; there are never to be two against one; and other rules, which soften the brutality of the art, and give to the very lowest, in their violence, some sort of generosity and honourable feelings. When two men are disposed to come to blows, nobody thinks of preventing them; but the populace make a ring, and see fair play. I was conducted a few days ago to Jackson's, a professor of pugilism, who keeps a school for the fashionables of London. He is the finest figure of a man I ever saw; all muscle; I could not clasp with my two hands the upper part of his arm, when the biceps was swollen by the contraction of the limb.*

Parliament has been employed this session on a very interesting subject. Sir Samuel Romilly, who is a very eminent lawyer, as well as a distinguished member of Parliament, but who is accused of thinking, with Lord Bacon, that time is the greatest of innovators, and that its suggestions should not be resisted, proposed to commute in certain cases capital punishment (death) for banishment and imprisonment. He wants also to define crimes more particularly than the laws do at present, and to circumscribe the arbitrary power of infliction given to the judge, and which extends at present from a few months imprisonment to the pain of death, for the same denomination of crime. The ancient criminal code of England is, he said, the most sanguinary in existence; it condemns to death a person stealing to the value of five shillings out of a shop or forty shillings out of a boat, or a public loading-place. There was a small majority against Sir Samuel Romilly's motion. He will bring on the question again in another shape, and good sense and justice must triumph at last.† Mr Windham spoke, as usual,

* John ("Gentleman") Jackson (1769–1845) was English champion from 1795 to 1803, although such was his enormous strength that he only had need to appear in the ring three times. One of his pupils who attended his school was Lord Byron.

† Sir Samuel Romilly (1757–1818), the great law reformer and passionate advocate of an abatement in the cruel severity of the Bloody Code, had introduced three Bills to limit capital punishment for crimes against property. After heated debates in the Commons and the Lords all the Bills were thrown

extremely well against the law as it is—and, at the same time, against its reformation.*

There is much to say against the custom of banishing criminals, particularly to such a prodigious distance as Botany Bay. The expence is enormous; it is a great charge upon the public; and the good citizens have a right to complain that rogues should be sent to travel at their expence. It may be, after all, a mistaken mercy to let them live. What a modern writer justly celebrated has said somewhat rigorously of the mere poor, might be said of these felons with much more propriety: "At nature's mighty feast there is no vacant seat for them." I own I did not expect to find here a system of criminal laws so inconsistent, so cruel, and at the same time so relaxed; and yet the end seems answered, for, with an unarmed police which is neither seen nor felt, there are no perceivable disorders, and no violence except those occasioned by political factions. Instead of the positive and unbending character generally ascribed to the English law, I find, that, in practice, it is arbitrary, and hardly under any other rule than the common sense of mankind. The noble institution of the jury on one hand, and on the other, the right of pardoning in the sovereign, correct all.

May 20.—We have made our first sortie from London, to see what the spring was out of its smoke and dust, 30 miles off, in the county of Surrey. The surface of the country is gently waving, covered with pasturage of the finest green, with numerous flocks of sheep, and herds of cattle; here and there groves of forest trees —but little arable land, few inclosures, and great heathy commons. All this is very beautiful, and pleases me extremely; but surprises me equally. So near this Colossus of a town, with its

---

out. Simond's hope that good sense and justice would triumph was unfounded. Romilly's Bill to repeal the Act which made the shoplifting of goods to the value of five shillings or more a capital offence was again defeated in the House of Lords in 1811, and then three more times in 1813, 1816, and 1818. In that last year his wife died and, overcome by grief and bitterly disappointed by his repeated defeats in Parliament, Romilly killed himself.

* William Windham (1750–1810), M.P. for Higham Ferrers, had formerly been Secretary of State for War and the Colonies. He shared Romilly's liberal views on most other political questions.

800,000 mouths to feed, I should have expected to see everywhere fields of corn for men, and of clover and sainfoin for animals; everywhere the plough—no trees but fruit-trees—no pastures, and, above all, no heath. We do not lose certainly by the exchange; but I do not understand how the proprietors of this valuable land calculate. I should suppose that all this beautiful country belongs to people of fortune, who think more of its beauty than its produce, and the conjecture is very much strengthened, by the appearance of multitudes of good-looking houses, half-mansion, half-cottage, but evidently inhabited by persons of taste and opulence.

I measured at Weston two *abeles* [white poplars] of twelve feet in circumference; several elms, and a young oak exceeded that size; the branches of a chesnut covered a space of a hundred feet in diameter.

I have been induced by the beauty of English lawns, to give some attention to the process of gardeners. The ground, ploughed and harrowed carefully, is either sown or sodded; rolling and mowing, and a moist climate do the rest, for there is nothing at all peculiar in the grass itself. The rolling is principally done in the spring, when the surface is sufficiently firm not to poach, and the bottom still yielding. If moss gets the better of the grass, ashes or fine mould restore it, but it is not to be done often, as the object is not to have the grass grow strong, but low and fine. The mowing, or rather shaving of this smooth surface, is done once a week, and even twice in warm rainy weather; once a month does in dry weather. The grass must be wet with dew or rain, and the scythe very sharp; the blade is wide, and set so obliquely on the handle, as to lye very flat on the sod. The rollers are generally of cast iron, 18 or 20 inches in diameter, and two and a half or three feet long, hollow, and weigh about 500 pounds, moved about by one man; those drawn by a horse are, of course, three or four times heavier. I have seen one, the diameter of which was seven or eight feet, and the weight 5000 or 6000 pounds, drawn by four horses.

June 2.—We are just returned from the naval hospital at Greenwich, on the Thames, five miles below London. It is a most beautiful edifice, singularly disposed . . . it is not only the most magnificent of hospitals, but the most cheerful I ever saw. It does not prevent, however, the old sailors who inhabit it from looking very tired and melancholy; they are seen warming themselves in the sun, or crawling languidly along the magnificent colonnades or porticoes, of which the elegance and beauty makes a sad contrast with their crippled, infirm, and dependent old age: 2400 of these veterans reside in the interior, 150 widows of sailors as nurses, and 200 sons of seamen, brought up for the navy. About 3000 out-pensioners receive L. 7 sterling a-year each. I have reason to believe, from some calculations made on the subject, that each of the 2400 house-pensioners costs, including the interest on the building, about L. 50 sterling a-year; and I believe that the out-pensioners, with their seven pounds a-year, which, without being sufficient, helps them to live, are vastly happier as long as they can do any work. Whatever the feelings of the veterans may be on the subject, there cannot be any doubt as to the impression which this noble and comfortable establishment must make on the young seamen passing before it, going up and down the Thames. "It is not," as [William] Paley rightly observes, "by what the Lord Mayor feels in his coach, but by what the apprentice feels who gazes at him, that the public is served."*

England has just lost Mr Windham. His death has been marked, as his life was, with the originality of his character. He would undergo a cruel operation, against the advice of medical men, and prepared himself with great courage, and a perfect knowledge of the danger, as appears by the letters he wrote, to be delivered in case of his death. It afforded, probably, the only chance for his life. Mr Windham has left a voluminous diary, which will be given to the public some time or other. This illustrious man has excited so general an interest, that it became necessary, in the last days of his illness, to satisfy the public by a daily bulletin. His sins are now forgiven, and all parties agree in doing justice to his perfect disinterestedness, his frankness, his generosity, his courage, his pro-

---

* Greenwich Hospital—begun in 1694 to the designs of Christopher Wren—was created in the grounds of the royal palace of Placentia as the naval equivalent of Chelsea Hospital. The Royal Naval College did not move there from Portsmouth until 1873.

found contempt of mere popularity, his knowledge, and eloquence. He leaves behind him no reputation equal to his; but he leaves many men capable of being more solidly useful than he was; and the state loses only a brilliant ornament. His fortune was about L. 6000 sterling a year, and all from patrimony—not acquired.

An event of another sort has divided public attention—the extraordinary attempt to assassinate one of the Princes, who was attacked in his bed, during the night, with his own regimental sabre, and escaped with difficulty, after receiving many wounds, none of which are mortal. One of his servants was found dead in an adjoining apartment, with a bloody razor not far from him, his throat cut from ear to ear, and he is supposed to be the assassin. This miserable man not having given before any marks of insanity, the motive of so desperate an act is become a great object of curiosity. He was an Italian.*

The birth-day, soon after this, has been celebrated with more than usual pomp.† The crowd was immense—the town illuminated—the people full of joy and loyalty—and on quite a cordial

* The Prince was the Duke of Cumberland (1771–1851) fifth son of George III; the servant a Piedmontese—some reports say a Corsican—valet named Sellis. It was widely believed at the time that Sellis had not cut his own throat but that the Duke had murdered him. There were rumours not only that the Duke had once been found in bed with Mrs Sellis but also that he was being blackmailed by her husband to whom he had made homosexual advances. There is a document in the Royal Archives, deposited there in the 1930's, which purports to be a "confession" by the Duke. A surgeon at the inquiry lent some weight to the theory of his guilt by testifying that Sellis, who was left-handed, could not have cut his throat in the way it was cut. On the other hand the foreman of the jury was Francis Place, a man in no way sympathetic to the Royal Family in general or to the Duke in particular; and the jury brought in a verdict of suicide. The most likely explanation seems to be that the Duke, a strange man of the most reactionary opinions, goaded Sellis into uncontrollable fury by taunting him with being a Roman Catholic.

† George III's birthday was on 4 June. His immediate successors were all born in the summer—George IV on 12 August, William IV on 21 August, Victoria on 24 May—so that it was usually found possible to have the sovereign's official birthday celebrations on the real birthday. Edward VII's birthday, however, was on 9 November so that in his reign it became customary to have the celebrations on a fixed date in June. Nowadays Queen Elizabeth's birthday (21 April) is celebrated on the second Saturday in June.

footing with the horse-guards on duty among them, which, considering the late tumults, and those expected shortly when Sir Francis Burdett comes out of the Tower, shews the English people to be, like all others, governed by the mere impulse of the moment. The ladies who go to court on the birth-day are dressed in the fashion of fifty years ago, as more suitable, I suppose, to the age of their majesties. They are carried there in sedan chairs, which can penetrate further than carriages; and it is really a curiosity to see them as they pass along the street towards the Palace of St James's. To enable them to sit in these chairs, their immense hoops are folded like wings, pointing forward on each side. The preposterous high head dress would interfere with the top, and must be humoured by throwing the head back; the face is therefore turned up, kept motionless in that awkward attitude, as if on purpose to be gazed at; and that face, generally old and ugly, (young women not going much there, it seems) is painted up to the eyes, and set with diamonds.

The glasses of the vehicle are drawn up, that the winds of Heaven may not visit the powder and paint too roughly; and this piece of natural history, thus cased, does not ill resemble a fœtus of a hippopotamus in its brandy bottle. The present generation can hardly believe that it was possible to be young and handsome in this accoutrement; and yet it was so. I have seen some of these ladies smile on the wondering spectators as they passed, conscious, I should hope, of their own absurd appearance.

June 6.—There has not been a drop of rain for the last six weeks; the verdure of the town gardens is destroyed, and the streets are very dusty, except the genteelest ones, which are inundated twice a-day by means of carts and fire-plugs communicating with the pipes under-ground, which circulate throughout the town. The windows are, however, universally adorned with plants quite fresh and luxuriant—the reseda particularly, which perfumes the air: this luxury is very general.

3

EAST ANGLIA, THE WEST COUNTRY AND WALES

12 June 1810 – 2 August 1810

June 12.—Oxborough, Norfolk.—We arrived here yesterday, 91 miles in a day and a half, counted for 95 miles, the fractions being always in favour of the horses. We had heard a bad character of this part of the country for beauty; but the chalky heaths about Newmarket have been much inclosed of late years in very large fields, and extensive screens of larches and pines, planted for the sake of timber, and protection against the east-winds; and, besides answering these good purposes, they are a great ornament. These easterly winds, which are cold and dry, are very apt to prevail on this coast, and are much dreaded; they have done a great deal of harm this spring. The first process of husbandry on a heath, consists in peeling off the surface, which is performed in a very laborious and awkward manner, by men pushing before them, by jerks of the middle part of the body, a very large sort of spade, sliding under the thin turf or heath, which is thrown up in heaps and burnt. It seems as if a machine might do this as well, with infinite saving of labour; but I dare say there is some good reason against it of which I am not aware. The scale of agriculture is such, that I saw five pair of fine horses with five harrows at work in one field. They sow their grain in drills, and weed it by means of a frame into which nine small hoes are inserted, alternately, in two rows, so as to run between nine lines or rows of plants at the same time; this weeding harrow is drawn by one pair of horses—enormous rollers are used to crush and pulverize the earth. The drought and night frost have done so much harm, that farmers are employed in many places in ploughing up their wheat to sow turnips. Large farm-houses are seen with all their out-houses substantial and complete—very few cottages. I do not know how and where the common labourers live, those in the fields do not appear poor or in rags—farmers on horseback ride about overlooking their labourers; they look like rich manufacturers, not at all like peasants.

Agriculture is evidently not a beggarly trade here. Large flocks of ragged sheep, with long black legs and noses, range about the heath, disputing with innumerable rabbits every blade of grass; the latter are seen popping in and out of their holes in every direction. The Norfolk sheep give the best English wool, next to the South Down; the price 35s. for 28 lb. No Merinos here. Rabbits sell at 6d. the carcass, and 1s. to 2s. 6d. the skin. Black-cattle here have no horns; of an accident they have made a species; I do not know whether there is any utility in it, but there certainly is no beauty.

About fifty miles from London, on a rising ground, we observed two barrows about 20 feet high, and near them a deep trench across the plain; these mounds are probably of Danish origin, covering heaps of bones of the slain in battle.

June 18.—Bury St Edmonds. The country we have passed is much the same as described before, chalk and flints, with a thin layer of vegetable soil—immense fields, without inclosures of any sort—no buildings in sight. Some parts of these plains give the idea of the sea. Farming is conducted in the same extensive style. We observed ten ploughs at work together in the same field, with each a pair of very fine horses—no oxen used in agriculture. Few villages, and those by no means pretty; but no appearance of poverty. The houses, indeed, poor enough on the outside—but the casements in good repair—the floors clean—and the people with decent working-clothes on, and healthy looks. No beggars at all to be seen. The roads, made of pounded flint, are hard and smooth—the horses fly along. It is certainly a pleasurable sensation to be thus transported with ease and swiftness, and without fatigue or exertions—a lazy sort of selfish pleasure, however, which one feels almost ashamed of enjoying.

The prices are here, for bread, 14½d. the quartern loaf of five lb.; beef, 9d. to 10d.; mutton, 9d.; veal, 8d. (this is the cheap time of veal); pork, 10s. for 14 lb.; all these are nearly London prices—Labour by the week in summer, 14s.; in winter, 12s. Workmen find themselves even in small beer. Women 8d. a-day.

After spending three days agreeably at Bury St Edmonds, we continued our journey towards London, by Cambridge. I am inclined to think English society pleasantest out of London. There is more leisure—as much information, and manners equally good; for nobody is provincial in this country. You meet nowhere with those persons who never were out of their native place, and whose habits are wholly local—nobody above poverty who has not visited London once in his life; and most of those who can, visit it once a year. To go up to town from 100 or 200 miles distance, is a thing done on a sudden, and without any previous deliberation. In France, the people of the provinces used to make their will before they undertook such an expedition.

There are almost everywhere book-societies or clubs, variously constituted. They are generally composed of ten or twelve persons, contributing annually a certain sum for the purchase of books. Any of them may propose a book, which, when read by all the associates who choose, is put up for sale among them. The person who recommended the purchase is obliged to take it at half price, if no one bids higher. The annual contribution is commonly from one to four guineas.

We visited Cambridge on our way to London. The University library is very large, and contains 90,000 volumes. Dr Clarke,* whose voyages are before the public, has enriched this university with antique marbles, rare manuscripts, and plants; and he has deposited in the library a very curious cast of Charles XII, the mould having been taken on his face four hours after his death at Frederickshall. The hole made by the ball is visible a little above the right eye. The mouth has a remarkable expression of contempt, and, upon the whole, it much resembles the portraits seen of him. I was employed in sketching this cast, when one of the under librarians objected to the thing being done, without permission being previously obtained. Another, however, stepped forth in defence of the arts, and said the permission was not necessary. During the altercation resulting from this conflict of authorities, I

* Edward Daniel Clarke (1769–1822). As travelling tutor to noblemen on the Grand Tour he visited most countries in Europe, also in the Middle East. In 1808 he was appointed first Professor of Mineralogy at Cambridge. The first of the six volumes of his *Travels* had just been published.

finished my sketch, which is very like; and did not fail to shew my gratitude to the good-natured librarian.

Some miles beyond Cambridge we found, at one of the inns, a boy of eighteen, seven feet nine inches high! I had never seen a giant, and had no idea of the effect. When sitting, his chair seemed likely to be crushed by his weight, as well as the table on which he rested his elbow; his feet and hands were particularly enormous; and when he rose, and crossed the room in two strides, with his head appearing to touch the ceiling, it was still more extraordinary—a person above the middle size could easily pass under his arm. This monstrous disproportion with surrounding objects overthrew all received ideas, almost as much as if houses had been seen moving, and dogs and horses with wings flying in the air. If this appears an exaggeration, I can only refer to a sight of my giant. He confessed that he could not lift a greater weight than another man, and a walk of four or five miles was a good deal for him. His voice is strong, but without being in proportion to his body; big bones, but not yet well covered with muscles, and he did not look as if he had done growing. He does not eat much; his large mild eyes look heavy, but he spoke sensibly. He told us that his father and mother, brothers and sisters, were all of common size.

June 29.—London, after such a long residence in it, appears like a sort of home; we are preparing, however, to leave it for a very long tour, by the West of England, Scotland, and return by the East. Aliens are required in time of war to apply at the alien-office, every three months, for a license to reside; a person of the country must join in the application. For such a journey as ours I have been required to name the principal places through which we are to pass, which does not exactly agree with our wandering plans, and threatens difficulties. I am far from blaming any proper precautions; but there seems to be very little to fear here from spying, or from a surprise; the publicity of every thing renders the one useless, and the sea renders the other impossible.

Sir William Petty indulged himself in speculations on the future increase of London, and found, that, in 1802, London would contain 5,359,000 inhabitants, and all England 9,825,000. This last prediction has been very curiously confirmed by the event, for in

1802 the census gave 9,706,378 for England and Wales; but, far from finding such an enormous proportion of that population accumulated in the capital in 1802, we find only 899,439; therefore the increase of London, however great, has advanced at a very retarded rate, and it will be more and more retarded. It is very possible that England might support twice its present number of inhabitants, considering the great quantity of uncultivated land; but these lands are probably inferior in quality, and might require twice the number of labourers sufficient for the good lands now in culture; therefore, although the population of England might double, that of the towns could not possibly; and there is no risk in predicting, that the population of London will never exceed a million and a half, and the other towns in proportion.*

July 6.—Salisbury is a little old city, very ugly, and of which there is nothing to say, except that the steeple of its cathedral, which is immensely high, and built of stone to its very summit, is twenty inches out of the perpendicular, which is really enough to take off the attention of the most devout congregation. We went to the morning service, and did not find a single person in the church except those officiating. It is not the first time we have observed this desertion of the metropolitan churches—even where the steeples were quite perpendicular. This church seems to lose in zeal and fervour what the sectaries have gained; and the regular clergy are accused of giving themselves too little trouble in the cause.

Three miles beyond Salisbury we visited Wilton, Lord Pembroke's. It is an old house, built in part by Inigo Jones. A whole wing was dismantled and thrown open ten years ago, to make a gallery of antiques. The floors, exposed to the injuries of the weather, are half rotten, and the poor antiques, thrown about higgledy piggledy, sans nose, sans fingers, sans every other prominent member, form a marble field of battle, half melancholy, half

---

* Sir William Petty (1623–1687) made his predictions in 1682. Although the population of London did not increase as rapidly as he forecast, by 1837 it had grown to two million, by 1851 to three and a quarter million and by the end of the century to five million. In 1871 London already contained almost as many people as all the urban areas of England and Wales had done fifty years before.

ridiculous, the sight of which would distress me beyond measure, were I their master, and could not afford to finish the work so unfortunately begun. Sancho might well have said here, "*qui trop embrasse mal étreint*".* Had the antiques been simply arranged along the walls of the apartments as they happened to be, without tearing down doors and windows, it would have been an interesting and respectable sight, which the possessor and the public would have enjoyed all this time. The site is low and flat; a velvet lawn, level as a piece of water unites to a real piece of water, artificial, and by no means bright, but of a good effect notwithstanding, and prodigious fine trees everywhere. They are such as are met with nowhere in the world except in an English park.

I measured an evergreen oak (not a large tree naturally); it covered a space of seventeen paces in diameter, and the trunk was twelve feet in circumference. An elm was sixteen feet in circumference, and many appeared about equal. Beyond the water, which before it spreads out into a stagnant lake, is a lively stream, you see an insulated hill covered with wood. We went to it by a very beautiful bridge. The view from that eminence is fine, and its slope would have afforded a healthier and pleasanter situation for the house. The deer came to the call, and ate leaves held to them—too tame for beauty, as they lose by it their graceful inquietude and activity, and become mere fat cattle for the shambles. Deer are a good deal out of fashion, and have given way to sheep in many parks.

From Wilton we went to Stourhead. The inn, close to the grounds, is in a romantic little lane, buried in laurels and pine

* At the time of Simond's visit, Wilton House was being altered by James Wyatt for the 11th Earl of Pembroke who wanted a more convenient house and more room for the family pictures and statuary and for the items he himself had acquired during and since his Grand Tours. Wyatt, who undertook far more work than he could properly supervise, was particularly neglectful of Wilton House where owing to poor construction, bad foremen and clerks of works, much of the new work had to be pulled down and started again at a final cost of £60,000. Wyatt was dismissed by Lord Pembroke in 1811, and the alterations were completed in 1814 by his nephew Jeffrey who, as Sir Jeffrey Wyatville, later became George IV's architect at Windsor.

trees, with a picturesque little Gothic church, all grey and mossy. After dinner, we were conducted to the house of Sir Richard Hoare. You go up a number of steps, too many by half, to the door, and enter a fine hall, leading to a large room in front, probably sixty by forty feet, and on each side a wing connected with the hall, by a short gallery. These apartments are full of pictures, none of which are very remarkable. One of the ladies and myself having sat down a moment to look at a picture more conveniently, a young girl who showed the house, told us as civilly as she could, that it was *the rule of the house not to allow visitors to sit down*. This is a rule of which that gentleman (a rich banker) has the merit of the invention. We have not met with any thing of the sort anywhere else; and there really seems to be less reason for it out of London, and in a place rather out of direct roads.*

The upper part of the grounds is very high, scooped out in the middle by a gentle descent, which becomes a deep dell or valley, where several springs unite to form the head of the Stour—a rapid little river. The grandfather of the present possessor dammed up this valley, which became a little irregular-shaped lake, covering perhaps thirty acres; the outlet, a fall of about twenty feet; the whole surrounded with woody banks and sloping lawns. Three temples peep out of the woods, marking the best points of view. An easy path leads to these stations, round the lake, passing by several fine springs, issuing clear and cool from the bosom of the mountain—one of them in a grotto. There is certainly great beauty in all this; but the water of the lake is dull and muddy, full of reeds and aquatic plants, which mark its stagnation. The lawns are half covered and belittled by shrubs, planted everywhere, particularly endless tufts and thickets of laurels; beautiful in themselves, but in too great profusion. The woods also are too close, resembling rather an American thicket. None of those magnificent single trees,

---

* Stourhead was built for Henry Hoare in 1722 by Colen Campbell. The grounds, of which Simond entertains so poor an opinion, were the first attempt to realise on English soil the idyllic scenery of the Italian romantic landscape painters. The house and grounds, now the property of the National Trust, are still open to the public.

so peculiar to English landscape, are to be seen here; in fact, I think there is as much done to spoil, as to adorn this fine spot. I have not yet seen an artificial piece of water that bore any resemblance to the water of a natural lake, always so clear; and it seems strange. Perhaps if the surface of a valley intended to be flooded, which is generally a rich soil, was first peeled off a few inches, or spade deep, according to the depth of the mould, aquatic plants would not be so apt to grow in the poor under-soil; worms and insects also would not meet with so much food as among the decayed sod and vegetable mould. The Serpentine River in Hyde Park is, I think, the clearest artificial water I have seen.

July 7.—After going the same round again this morning, we left Stourhead for Bristol, 37 miles of most beautiful country; a continual garden, full of gentlemen's houses and grounds, and of neat cottages, single, and in villages; too much chequered with inclosures for picturesqueness; but exhibiting every appearance of prosperity. The road very hilly, but in perfect repair, and the horses excellent, as we have found them everywhere, except in Cornwall and Devonshire. The multitude of gentlemen's houses, scattered over the country, is a feature quite peculiar to English landscape. The thing is unknown in France, where the country, at a distance from large towns, presents only farm-houses and peasants' cottages, and now and then a castle, old and neglected; but none of these houses which are the habitual residence of comfort and elegance. In France, the landed-proprietors have their houses in the nearest little town.

July 9.—Bristol. As we get farther from London, I think I perceive more moderation in political opinions; fewer people speak of revolution, either to wish or fear it, or believe the people ripe for it. The party of which Cobbett is the mouth-piece, does not appear numerous out of the capital. Mixed with abundance of undeniable facts, and under the garb of downright truth and honest surliness, Mr Cobbett deals out principles the most fallacious, with great art, and wonderful force of popular eloquence; but his frequent and outrageous contradictions of his own principles have, in a great degree, neutralized them. He is to receive judgment this day, having been tried for a libel, with intention to excite the troops to mutiny.*

There is not another government in Europe who could long withstand the attacks to which this is continually exposed. The things published here would set on fire any other heads in the world; but either from insensibility, reason, or habit, they make but little impression.

From our hotel at Bristol we see and hear continually the troops quartered here exercising on the square before the cathedral. There are five regiments, principally employed in guarding a depot of prisoners of war. The soldiers, compared at least to the guards in London, are by no means stout-looking. The officers are in general larger made than the men; and this is a confirmation of what I think I have observed before, that the class of gentlemen in England is a finer race of men than the same class in France; but there is not the same difference between the common people of the two countries respectively.

We have had several days in June and July, called here very warm, which may be considered as a fair sample of English summer heat, and that was quite moderate, compared to the heat in America. The climate, both winter and summer, is never extreme; and although rarely resplendent, is best for use, more favourable for exercise, either for labour or pleasure. The people, accordingly, are visibly more active here than in America.

July 11.—Ross. We left our carriage this morning at Chepstow, near the mouth of the Wye, and came to this place in a hired chaise, proposing to return by the river; 31 miles of very fine but very hilly country. From a height we had an extensive view of a most rich tract, the Vale of Monmouth, twenty miles every way, and cultivated like a garden. Farms in it let for L.5 and L.6 an acre; forty years ago the rent of the same land did not exceed 30s. or 40s. an acre: it belongs mostly to the Duke of Beaufort. Soon after, from another height, the Vale of Usk, nearly as rich, but mostly meadow, being overflowed every spring. At Ragland [Rag-

* Judgement was given against him. He was fined £1,000 and imprisoned for two years. He was in Newgate when Simond visited the prison the following September.

lan] we visited the ruins of the castle of that name, the last subdued by the cannon of Cromwell. The floors and roofs are of course gone, but enough of the walls remain to trace a large hall, perhaps 50 by 30 feet, and 25 feet high, with spacious bow-windows (the frames of stone are yet entire), looking over a spacious court, and an enormous fire-place, with double flues forking off, with a window between, just above the fire—the music-gallery, and drawing-room; then, under the keep, the subterraneous dungeons, where prisoners were let down by a sort of well, and the very "loop-hole grates where captives weep" still perfectly visible. We felt no kind of compassion for the decay of this goodly castle—it is better as it is than it was; and the comparison between the times of its glory and the present make the existing grievances appear very light. Some of the towers are entire, and ivy is mantling over the whole, according to the best rules of picturesqueness.

Wishing to see the last number of Cobbett, we sent the servant of the inn to procure it; he is just returned, and informs us, that nobody in Chepstow knows anything of Cobbett's Political Register. I do not know whether to wish the good people of Chepstow joy of it, or to pity them; as the Political Register, together with some treason, contains certainly a good deal of information and entertainment.

July 14.—We are at Cowbridge, Glamorganshire. Forty miles to-day, through Newport, Cardiff, and Landaff—the country just uneven enough to afford extensive views over an immense extent of cultivation, lost in the blue distance; nothing wild, or, properly speaking, picturesque, but all highly beautiful, and every appearance of prosperity. Wales seems more inhabited, at least more strewed over with habitations of all sorts, scattered or in villages, than any part of England we have seen, and which are rendered more conspicuous by white-washing of the most resplendent whiteness. Every cottage too has its roses, and honeysuckles, and vines, and neat walk to the door; and this attention bestowed on objects of mere pleasurable comforts, is the surest indication of minds at ease, and not under the immediate pressure of poverty. It is impossible indeed to look round without the conviction, that this country is, upon the whole, one of the happiest, if not the happiest in the world. The women we see are certainly better looking than nearer London. The language of the inhabitants is quite unintelligible to us; at the inns, however, all is transacted in English. Having gone to see some ruins while the horses were changing at Cardiff, we found the post-boy had driven away; and on inquiring the reason on his return, he said he was afraid the horses would catch cold standing—this is delightful for the middle of July, when the people of New York are dying with heat.

July 16.—Tenby. Ninety-one miles in two days, through a hilly but rich country, affording continually vast views of cultivation, a surface chequered with fields and hedges, and studded over with white dots, the outside of cottages, roofs and chimneys, and even the very stones on the road near the houses being fresh whitewashed.

Near Swansea we visited the copper and iron works. They were just opening a smelting furnace; the fused copper, in a little stream of liquid fire, flowed along a channel towards a cistern full of water; we saw it approach with terror, expecting an explosion; instead of which the two liquids met very amicably, the water only simmering a little. The workmen looked very sickly: we found, on inquiry, their salary was but little higher than that of common labourers. It is remarkable, that, much as men are attached to life, there is no consideration less attended to in the choice of a profession than salubrity.

July 20.—Aberystwith. Another stage of 40 miles with four horses, in ten hours. There is so little travelling in this remote part of the island, that the post-horses are commonly employed in husbandry. The country is rough and hilly, but presents the same appearance of prosperity and good cultivation, though less fertile; granite and slate having succeeded to limestone. The country people give us a friendly nod as we drive along. The women certainly are uncommonly good-looking. Welsh for two shillings is *dua sols*, as we hear it pronounced, which sounds very like French.

July 25.—We left Tan-y-Bwlch this morning with three horses, and the next stage with two, after being obliged to take four for the preceding 210 miles. We passed to Beddgelert, Carnarvon, and Bangor Ferry—this last is the place for embarkation for Ireland, by Anglesey. We have stopped for the night at a country inn eight miles beyond, superlatively comfortable, and with the finest view possible. It is not a post-house; but finding the house at Bangor Ferry full, and no horses, those of Carnarvon have brought us so far, and we have sent forward for others. Post-horses do not seem under many regulations; the price, &c. appear left to the natural operation of competition; and in remote places where post-horses are kept by one person only, the traveller is pretty much at his mercy. I have, however, experienced so little difficulty in our already extensive travels, that I have not yet taken the trouble of ascertaining whether there is any legal check to exactions; the fact is, that there is less disposition to it, a more accommodating temper, and civility of behaviour among the people, than, not only in America, but in France, as far as I recollect. A pair of horses is generally 1s. 6d. per mile, sometimes 1s. 3d. or 1s. 4d.; leaders, when necessary, only 1s. per mile; postilions about $2\frac{1}{2}$d. per mile. Ferries are extremely high: the passage of Conway river costs 16s. while the ferry across the North river at New York, four times as wide, costs about one half of that sum.

July 26.—This moderate climate is certainly much fitter for bodily exercise than that of America. We think nothing of five or six miles a-day on foot. The flies, however, begin to be almost as numerous and inconvenient out of doors as there, but not in the house. Musketoes are by no means unknown. We see snakes, but the viper is the only one deemed dangerous. America is usually thought to be full of these reptiles, and that you are exposed every moment to tread upon a rattle-snake; the fact is, that the sight of a snake is not much more common there than here, and most of them are as harmless. A child armed with a stick will attack and kill the rattle-snake, which is very sluggish—it is met only in dry stony places. The snakes of moist places are not venomous.

July 28.—We travelled to-day from Ruthven along the vale of Clwydd, and, ascending the rampart of the hills which encloses it, we admired, for the last time, this magnificent extent of cultivation. On the brow of a neighbouring hill, and threatening the valley, which the Abbey seemed to enjoy, appeared the wall of Dinas Bran, or Crow Castle. The area of Valle Crucis Abbey now encloses a grove of lofty ash trees, which overtop the ruins, and have a fine and singular effect; so interwoven are the roots and ruins, that stones appear to grow out of the trees, as well as trees out of the stones. Some peasants have taken up their abode among the remains of the cloisters; cows and hogs, chickens and children, climb and perch on the trees and ruins, and you may see here a pair of horns, there a child's head or a pig's peeping through the windows, among Gothic carvings and green boughs.

July 29.—From Llangollen, by Wrexham and Chester, 46 miles.

At Chester we visited the court-house and prison of the county—a new building of classical appearance, the interior of which is on a plan of the celebrated philanthropist (not of the sort of those who made the French revolution) Howard.* This is its plan. The windows of the apartments of the keeper overlook the rooms or cells of the prisoners which are disposed in a semicircle, opening two and two on a small court or garden, to which they have access all day, and are only shut up at night. A list, placed on the balcony before the windows of the keeper, informs you of the name of each prisoner, his crime, &c. The court forms also a semicircle—the judge and jury in the centre—the spectators on the stone amphitheatre all around. The prisoner is brought by a subterraneous passage to his place before the judges. The court is lighted by a sky-light, with ventilators to renew the air. The front of the building is adorned by a Doric portico, the columns of which, three feet in diameter, and twenty high, are each formed of a single piece, and the whole building of the same stone, in large blocks, of a fine yellow colour, from a quarry near at hand. The funds have been drawn from the surplus produce of a canal in the neighbourhood beyond a certain per centage stipulated in the charter. What pleased us most was, to find that this excellent house had so few inhabitants; and the jailor, who appeared to be a respectable man, informed us further, that there had been only three executions in the county of Chester in nine years.

The city of Chester has an antique physiognomy, not exactly of

* John Howard (1726–90) had published his classic work, *The State of the Prisons in England and Wales* in 1777. Chester Prison was one of the earliest to be built upon the plan which he, and later Jeremy Bentham, advocated.

classical, but rather barbarous antiquity. The streets are in the houses—that is to say, that the ground-floor is hollow, and open to the public—a sort of covered gallery, dark, dirty, and crooked, and up and down, with unexpected steps, down which you run the risk of falling every moment. The origin of this singular style of architecture goes back to the times when the neighbouring Welsh made inroads on the frontier town of Chester, when the inhabitants defended themselves to advantage from their galleries. They are still of great use against an enemy, to whose attacks they are as much exposed to as ever—frequent rains.

We finished our day's journey by crossing the river, or rather arm of the sea, at Liverpool—a long, inconvenient, and expensive ferry, (28s.) and we have been landed on the quay of this great town with our carriage without horses, without knowing where to find any, where to go, or to whom to apply. After some unsuccessful attempts to procure private lodgings, we were obliged to put up at the Liverpool Arms, a sort of Noah's ark, like all great inns in sea-port towns.

Liverpool a good deal resembles New York. The latter town is larger, (96,000 inhabitants, instead of 80,000), and perhaps better built as to common dwellings; but the public buildings of Liverpool are more numerous, and in a better style of architecture.*
There are several literary establishments, with respectable libraries, in large and convenient apartments, and well attended by the inhabitants of this great commercial town, who are not nearly so exclusively merchants as those on the western continent.

August 2.—We slept yesterday at Ormskirk, thirteen miles from Liverpool, and did not lose by the change. The local militia was assembled, and looked full as well as troops of the line, performing their exercise with great precision; they were not however very fine men. The females of this part of the country (Lancashire) seem gifted with a larger share of beauty than the men. We meet with many pretty faces, and fine shapes. This evening we are at Kendal; 63 miles to-day through a very fine country. Not the least appear-

---

* Liverpool was "one of the best built towns" that John Wesley had ever seen. It had grown rich on the profits of the slave trade; and the Irish immigration, which was to give rise to its Victorian slums, had not yet begun.

ance of poverty anywhere. The people at work in the fields, making hay, are all decently clothed. The cottages, though meanly built, mostly with mud, and thatched, have good casements; whitewashed inside; roses and honeysuckle against the wall, and even jessamines and geraniums. This surely indicates a great degree of ease and comfort among the lower ranks. We passed, in the course of the day, immense fields of potatoes; the blossoms of some fields all purple, and others all white. Wheat seems cultivated on a smaller scale. Indeed I have not seen anywhere, in England, those boundless fields of waving corn, so common in the north of France. There is, on the other hand, much more land in meadows. Judging by their fields, they should consume more meat than bread in this country.

We have crossed many canals to-day, or perhaps the same several times over, on very good stone bridges of a single arch. These canals wind round hills, following levels, like natural streams, and are not at all offensive, in a picturesque light, except when they happen sometimes to travel side by side with a real river.

The common people here, as well as everywhere in England, are very willing to answer questions to the best of their abilities, but they seem to know less beyond their immediate calling than the same classes in America—the farmer knows nothing beyond the plough—the shopman out of his trade—and the post-boy only that part of the road to the next stage.

We slept at *merry* Carlisle (dull and ugly enough), 42 miles; and to-day, by Longtown and Langholm, to Hawick, 44 miles. About twelve miles north of Carlisle, our post boy shewed us a tree which divides the two kingdoms; a nominal division, which brings to mind forcibly the unhappy times when this very frontier was a desert, called debateable lands, open to the reciprocal depredations of the lawless borderers on both sides, and that little more than one hundred years ago.

4

SCOTLAND
2 August 1810 – 20 February 1811

August 2.—We passed this afternoon a tract of country very different from England. It is a succession of steep hills, with intervening vallies, all uniformly covered with a fine green turf, smooth, and unbroken by a single tree, bush, weed, or stone; sheep hanging along the sides of the acclivities, and here and there a shepherd-boy wrapped up in his plaid—nothing to interrupt the sameness and stillness, but the little stream bustling along each valley, over a bed of round pebbles. The Scotch are said to be more industrious and more thrifty than the Welsh. They cannot afford leisure, I suppose, to be comfortable, and certainly do not ruin themselves by luxuries. Children, in health and in rags, with fair hair and dirty faces, swarm on the dunghills at each door. An old barrel stuck through the thatch serves for a chimney. The stable and dwelling are under the same roof; one door serves for both—and the dark *runnings* from the heap of dung, and the heap of peat, piled up against the house, drain under the floor, and some upon it. The climate must be healthy indeed, where all this does not breed infection. The fields of potatoes and oats seem in the best state, and the people are making hay everywhere.

We meet with strings of light one horse carts, driven by only one man—a much better contrivance than the English heavy waggons. The men along the roads have generally the plaid thrown across their shoulder, and over one arm. Some wear it like a Spanish cloak, or an antique drapery, and, with their short petticoat and naked knees, might be mistaken for Roman soldiers, if the vulgar contrivance of hat and shoes did not betray the northern barbarian. The females have their extremities more classical, for they go barefooted and bareheaded, and only fail by the middle, covered with vile stiff stays and petticoats. We see them at the fords of their little brooks, exhibiting, very innocently I believe, higher than the knee, unmindful of the eye of travellers.

August 10.—Edinburgh, by Selkirk, 47 miles. We have crossed to-day the Tweed, the Etterick, and the Yarrow, the names of which sound poetical in our ears.

This is a town of 90 or 100,000 inhabitants (the tenth part of London), in three distinct divisions; the old and the new town side by side, with the wide ditch between; then the port, (seaport) at about a mile distance, on the Firth of Forth. The shops, tradesmen, and labourers, are mostly in the old town. The college is there also, but learning begins to be attracted by politeness, and the professors come to live in the region of good dinners and fine ladies.

August 18.—We have just seen the penitentiary house, constructed on a very ingenious plan—a semicircular building, seven stories high, each containing fourteen cells, all open towards the common centre, which is like a great well open from top to bottom. A bow window, with lattices, repeated at each story, overlooks them all, and nothing can be done by the prisoners without being seen; they work solitary, and in silence, in these 98 cells; and at night sleep in other little rooms behind them. This tower, or rather section of a tower, is lighted by a sky light, and well ventilated. No bad smells—no noise—great order—all as well as possible; except that the correction does not correct; and the same individuals are observed to return from time to time to enjoy again this philosophical retirement. A thing happened to us here which deserves to be mentioned. I had observed written over the door, an injunction not to give any money; but the woman who conducted us was so obliging, that I could not believe she did not expect some recompense for her trouble, and she received what I gave her without saying any thing; but when, on leaving the house, I was going to put something into the box for poor prisoners, the keeper said it was unnecessary, as the woman who had accompanied us had just put in the half crown I had given her! We had not seen her do it; she had disappeared immediately, and could have no motive of ostentation; nobody was present when she received the money. "*Où la vertu va-t-elle se nicher!*"

A large and convenient house in the best part of Edinburgh (Queen Street) built of freestone, has just been sold for L. 3000; another nearly equal, for L. 2500; and in inferior streets, very good houses may be had for L. 1800, or hired for L. 100 a-year, and about L. 30 taxes. A manservant L. 40 a-year; a woman-cook L. 12; a maid-servant L. 8. A carriage, including coachman, and every thing else, L. 250 a-year.

During the nine days we have spent at Edinburgh, there has not been a single one without some showers of rain; but we are told it is after a long drought. The temperature of the air varies from 60° to 72°. It is strange to see the women going about the streets barefooted, on the pavement, which is very smooth, but continually wet; they are in other respects cleanly dressed, even with gloves on, and an umbrella. The fish-market is supplied by women, who come some miles with enormous loads of fish on their backs, strapped across the breast. Their husbands are out all night in their boats, catching these fish, with which the women leave home at break of day. They look strong, healthy, and very cheerful, singing along the road; but in general remarkably ugly; and among the lower people in Scotland, the sex is certainly not beautiful.

We have reason to be grateful for the hospitality shewn us at Edinburgh, and we do not leave it without regret.

August 21.—At Lanark, we stopped a moment at a cotton-manufactory. It was the first established in Scotland, and the most considerable. It is certainly a prodigious establishment. We saw four stone buildings, 150 feet front each, four stories high of twenty windows, and several other buildings, less considerable— 2500 workmen, mostly children, who work from six o'clock in the morning till seven o'clock in the evening, having in that interval an hour and a quarter allowed for their meals; at night, from eight to ten for school. These children are taken into employment at eight years old, receiving five shillings a-week; when older, they get as much as half-a-guinea. Part of them inhabit houses close to the manufactory, others at Lanark, one mile distance; and we were assured the latter are distinguished from the others by healthier looks, due to the exercise this distance obliges them to take—four miles a day. Eleven hours of confinement and labour, with the schooling, thirteen hours, is undoubtedly too much for children. I think the laws should interfere between avarice and nature. I must acknowledge, at the same time, that the little creatures we saw did not look ill.

We set out from Lanark on foot, to visit, in our way, the course of the Mouse, an imperceptible little river, at the bottom of a frightful chasm, quite out of sight and hearing, from the great depth of its banks. The path along the top is, in some places, so narrow and slippery, as to make you cling to the trees and bushes instinctively. We were shewn, by the guide, the very place where the hounds of his Grace of Hamilton, in close pursuit of a fox, rushed down a precipice of five hundred and some feet after him (the height was measured after the event) and caught the fox in the water, into which they all fell! The guide next shews you, among the rocks on the opposite side, a dark hole leading to a cavern, the hiding-place (he had many) of the Caledonian hero, Wallace; then the place where, quite lately, an adventurous boy was let down by a rope held by two other boys, some hundred feet along the surface of a bald rock, to get at a nest of grey hawks, which they sold for fifteen shillings!

August 24.—On our arrival in Glasgow this morning, we found at the inn several notes of invitation, and offers of service, as obliging as unexpected. We have seen carding and spinning-mills, weaving-mills, mills for everything. The human hand and human intelligence are not separated; and mere physical force is drawn from air and water alone, by means of the steam-engine. Manufactories, thus associated with science, seem to produce with the facility and fecundity of nature. It is impossible to see without astonishment these endless flakes of cotton, as light as snow, and as white, ever pouring from the carding-machine, then seized by the teeth of innumerable wheels and cylinders, and stretched into threads, flowing like a rapid stream, and lost in the *tourbillon* of spindles. The eye of a child or of a woman watches over the blind mechanism directing the motions of her whirling battalion, rallying disordered and broken threads, and repairing unforeseen accidents. The shuttle likewise, untouched, shoots to and fro by an invisible force; and the weaver, no longer cramped upon his uneasy seat, but merely overlooking his self moving looms, produces forty-eight yards of cloth in a day, instead of four or five yards.

Sept. 1.—To Killin, only 21 miles to-day, through much the same sort of country as yesterday; glen after glen—green, and bare, and deserted, with towering hills all round; one of them seemed to have the form of an immense crater—a hollow cup—but all the detached masses below were granite and schistus, and nothing volcanic. Beautiful pieces of quartz lay about everywhere. Some of the hills could not be less than 2000 feet high. The Tay, an inconsiderable mountain torrent, descended with us the whole day. The question occurs naturally in traversing these solitudes, where are the men? Where are the Highlanders? And if you are told that the system of sheep-farming has banished them from their country, then you would be apt to ask, where are the sheep? Very few indeed are seen; the grass is evidently not half eaten down—hardly touched, indeed, in many places. We met to-day, however, with several habitations, and we entered some of them; a small present was willingly received, and served as a passport to our curiosity. The only door is common to men and beasts, and, of course, very dirty. You see, as you come in, on one side a small stable, which seems very unnecessary, since, in the much more rigorous climate of North America, cattle have commonly no shelter in winter. The other side is separated by a rough partition; this is the dwelling-place of the family; you find in it not a chimney, but a fire-place on the ground, with a few stones round it, immediately under a hole in the roof; a hook and chain fastened to a stick, to hang an iron kettle on; a deal table; a piece of board, on which oat-cakes are prepared; a dresser, with some little earthenware; an old press; a pickling-tub for mutton; some pieces of mutton hung in the smoke, which winds round them on its way to the roof; a shelf with many cheeses, and among the cheeses a few books. The beds were a filthy mattrass, and a filthy blanket—no sheets; no floor—only the ground trodden hard; a window of four small panes, not one entire. Such is the interior; and to finish the picture of these hovels, each has its ladder against the roof; either to stop the progress of fire, when the thatch happens to catch, or a leak, which they do by means of a few sods. Some of the roofs bore a luxuriant crop of grass. This is abject poverty, or at least appears so; yet these people feel no want, and enjoy health, which is more than many do who are rich. Their poverty does not seem to extend to food, for they have plenty of fish from their lakes and rivers; and one acre of potatoes can feed a family. They have also a small fields of oats; meat is not probably very scarce near such flocks of sheep, and I saw hogs to-day. Fuel is at their door. Labour is paid 2s. 6d. or 3s. a-day. With such means of subsistence, I do not understand what the Highlanders gain by migrating to America. With some labour, they can procure here, what is not to be had there without labour. There are schools here everywhere; children learn to read in English and Erse; but the last language alone is in common use.

September 2.—Taymouth, 16 miles to-day in five hours, the road ascending and descending continually along the banks, without any apparent use.

To-day being Sunday, the road was full of country people going to church, in their best clothes. They were all clean and decent. About half the men wore the kilt, and tartan hose, and plaid over their shoulders, and they looked best. The women by no means handsome, nor indeed the men, but healthy and active. The men generally touched their hats or highland bonnet, as they passed by us. We were rather ashamed of our Sunday travelling.

September 3.—Dunkeld, $23\frac{1}{2}$ miles. The Highlander, our guide, who was a very intelligent man, told us that his countrymen were very fond of whisky; that some working men could drink an English quart of it in a day, which costs 3s. 9d. They get only from 2s. to 3s. a-day when they work, and half that sum in winter—therefore cannot be supposed to indulge themselves very often with full allowance; but men able to bear that quantity of ardent spirits, must have practised much and often. Malt liquors are in use also, but whisky is preferred. I must own, however, that we have not yet met with a drunken man. Our guide differed from us on the subject of Highland cottages; which he maintained were quite good enough. The people do not feel, he said, the want of better dwellings; they would not be happier in them—and would cease to be the hardiest soldiers and sailors of Great Britain. We understood that some of the Highlanders who went to America, had returned, and many more would, if they had wherewithal to pay their pas-

Edinburgh: the Castle from Grassmarket

Staffordshire collieries

The Butcher Row, Exeter

A poor quarter in London

Scene in the Strand

A ward in Middlesex Hospital, London

sage. The rent of the worst huts, with a few roods of ground for potatoes, is often so low as 5s. a-year. They have a tax, (hearth-money), of 4s. 6d. a-year to pay, but it is not strictly levied. The window-tax does not begin at a less number than seven windows—which is quite beyond their mark. A horse under thirteen hands does not pay any tax, and one of that size would pass, in the Highlands, for a dromedary. We were even told that taxable horses instead of 12s. 6d., are reduced to 2s. 6d. in favour of small farmers, whose rent is below L. 10 sterling a-year. It appears to me, therefore, that the Highlanders pay no direct taxes; and of those on consumption, they do not seem liable to any but that on whisky.

Sept. 15.—Melrose, 34 miles. We set out from Edinburgh this morning, with the same fine weather which we have had constantly since we left the Highlands. The reapers are hard at work everywhere, with their sickles, an instrument vastly inferior to the cradle-scythe used in America, and of which the figure and description are annexed. We observed forty-five reapers in one field.

There are no stage-coaches in the Highlands. We now meet them on the roads, and the absurdity of their construction strikes us anew. There are twelve or fifteen persons on top, besides baggage, and accidents are frequent. These carriages, and the heavy waggons with conical wheels, ought not to be found in a country where the science and practice of mechanics are so well understood.

Sept. 19.—Windermere. We have scaled the ramparts of the mountains between Ulswater and Windermere, and admired again the wild magnificence of the pass, steeper and higher, perhaps, than any we have seen in Scotland. We shall rest here with our friends during the remainder of the fine autumnal weather, making only occasional excursions among the lakes and mountains, of which this is the centre.

There are no retired places in England, no place where you see only the country and countrymen; you meet, on the contrary, everywhere town-people elegantly dressed and lodged, having a number of servants, and exchanging invitations. England, in short, seems to be the country-house of London; cultivated for amusement only, and where all is subservient to picturesque luxury and ostentation. Here we are, in a remote corner of the country, among mountains, 278 miles from the capital—a place without commerce or manufactures, not on any high road; yet everything is much the same as in the neighbourhood of London. Land, half-rock, is bought up at any price, merely on account of the beauty of the spot. The complaints about scarcity of servants and labourers, and their consequent high prices, are general. It is plain there are too few poor for the rich. The latter talk of the weight of taxes as intolerable, and of the increase of price of everything as excessively alarming; while the poor seem to take all this very easily, increasing and multiplying; while the others decay and fall off continually.

The rich show certainly a very great eagerness to buy land, being a safe property, and a permanent revenue; and because there is really, notwithstanding the loud complaints, an inundation of wealth in the country. The effect of competition is to raise the price of land and of labour to such a degree, that the small landholders are tempted by the first, and indeed forced by the latter, to sell, and become simple farmers; swelling thus the number of those who have nothing to lose. This excessive concentration of tangible property is considered, by many well-informed people, as more dangerous, more conducive to a revolution, than the weight of taxes, or any of the other popular grievances.

Oct. 10.—Grasmere is the nearest lake to Windermere—an hour's walk across the hill, but much more by the road. It is a little pool surrounded by mountains nearly equal in height, sloping everywhere to the water's edge.

We were shown in the valley north west of Grasmere, a lone cottage, inhabited last winter by a peasant of the name of Green, his wife, and nine children. The father and mother had gone to a cattle fair in Langdale, separated from their vale by a mountain. There was a fall of snow. The evening came on, and they did not return. The youngest child was only a few months old, the eldest a girl about ten years old; she took care to feed the baby with a little milk which happened to be in the house. The next day she procured from a neighbouring farm some more milk. The father and mother not yet returned, another night passed in the same manner. The following day, the little girl going again for her supply of milk, was questioned—her situation discovered, and strong suspicions of the accident. The alarm spreading in the valley, fifty people set out to explore the hill, and soon discovered the bodies. It appears, that, having lost the track, the unfortunate couple had wandered higher up in the mountain; that the husband had fallen from a rock, and from appearances had died by the fall. The woman, warned by the fall, had reached the bottom of the rock by a circuitous way, and groped about for him a great while, the snow being all trodden down. She had lost her shoes, which were found in different places; and falling at last from fatigue and cold, died probably the easy death ordinary in such cases. Some persons thought afterwards they recollected having heard distant screams in the mountain during the storm, but they did not suspect the cause; nor, if they had, would they probably have been in time to give assistance. The bodies, followed by all the inhabitants of the valley, and by the nine orphans, were buried in the same grave. The latter have since been adopted, or at least taken care of by the people of the neighbourhood.

Some years before this, a sportsman perished in these mountains, in a manner still more tragical. A dog had been observed coming from time to time to the houses of the valley, and, after obtaining some food, returning to the mountains. He was at last followed, and the body of his master discovered. He had, it seems, dislocated his foot and, unable to move, had died of hunger and pain, and his faithful dog had ever since watched by his remains.

Oct. 15.—Windermere. We had the pleasure of seeing several times the celebrated Mr Southey, a distinguished favourite of the English muses, Mr Coleridge, whose talents are equally known, although less fruitful, was at Mr S.'s, with whom he had some family connection.* Both of these gentlemen, and, I believe, Mr Wordsworth, another of the poets of the lakes, had, in the warmth of their youthful days, some fifteen years ago, taken the spirited resolution of traversing the Atlantic, in order to breathe the pure air of liberty in the United States. Some accident delayed the execution of this laudable project, and gave them time to cool. At

* Robert Southey (1774–1843) and Samuel Taylor Coleridge (1772–1834) married the sisters Sara and Edith Fricker. For a time they all lived together, with a third sister, at Greta Hall, Keswick.

present, these gentlemen seem to think that there is no need of going so far for liberty, and that there is a reasonable allowance of it at home. Their democracy is come down to Whiggism, and may not even stop there. Mr S. has resided in Spain, and is well acquainted with the literature of that country, and its people. He thinks the Spaniards are well aware of the defects of their government, and that a thorough reformation of them, and in fact a revolution, would have united the whole people against the invaders, and have rendered them invincible. He and his friend are enthusiastic in the Spanish cause. This sentiment is, in them, I am persuaded, quite sincere, and founded on just and honourable principles. But it is remarkable, that this same Spanish cause is one of the watch-words of party, to which I have alluded before. By a strange perversion of the human mind, those liberal and independent opinions in matters of government, which one of the parties professes, are generally found associated with a certain toleration of usurpation and tyranny in certain situations; which is, on the contrary, held in utter abhorrence by the other party, although accused of being, otherwise, less nice on those points than its adversary. This might well raise uncharitable suspicions of the candour and sincerity of both.

We have just read in all the newspapers a full and disgusting account of the public and cruel punishment on the pillory of certain wretches convicted of vile indecencies. I can conceive nothing more dangerous, offensive, and unwise, than the brutality and unrestrained publicity of such infliction. The imagination itself is sullied by the exposition of enormities, that ought never to be supposed to exist; and what are we to think of a people, and women too, who can for hours indulge in the cowardly and ferocious amusement of bruising and maiming men tied to the stake, and perfectly defenceless! Thus taught, is it to be expected that they will always know how to distinguish between a legal atrocity, and another which is not so? and can there be a better school for hanging *à la lanterne*, or September massacres, whenever a fit opportunity shall occur? Tame tigers must not taste blood; and once let loose, cannot easily be muzzled again at pleasure. What a singular anomaly in a government of laws are these mob executions! It is scarcely more than half a century since the English drowned witches. In the year 1751, two old women, suspected of the black art, were taken up, and, in the course of certain experiments of the mob to try their guilt by immersion in a horse-pond, they were actually drowned, at a place called Tring, a few miles only from London.*

Nov. 17.—Edinburgh. We came here in three days, (140 miles). The roads are made of broken stones, hard, and jolting like a bad pavement, but without ruts. The heavy English waggons, with fellies to their wheels, 16 and 18 inches broad, would soon crush these asperities; in this respect, they are certainly preferable to the light one-horse carts used here.

Our entrance into Scotland was this time by Gretna-Green notorious for smuggled weddings. The marriage forms are very simple in Scotland. It is enough to aknowledge a woman as your wife before witnesses, and even enough to live apparently as married, to be so legally and indissolubly. In England, there are banns to be published in church, and other formalities, inconvenient to unauthorized lovers. I do not exactly know why this village has been chosen in preference to others on the frontier of Scotland, except its being the first on the road, and having acquired, by prescription, the good-will of the trade. We inquired of our landlady about the old drunken blacksmith, said to be the high priest of this fugitive hymen. She denied, however, indignantly his having ever been a blacksmith. He is likely to die soon from age and drinking; and then our informant added, with a sigh, "What will become of *us, God only knows!*" No less than a hundred couple have been conjoined here annually. We might have been admitted to the sight of this noble personage for a glass of grog. He is neither a clergyman nor a magistrate, but reads the English marriage-service to tranquillize the scruples of the lady, and persuade her

* The statutes against witchcraft were repealed in 1736 but less than twenty years before a girl of eleven was hanged, together with her mother, for having sold her soul to the Devil and caused her neighbours to vomit pins. As late as the 1760's country women were still being thrown into ponds with their thumbs and toes tied together to undergo the ancient test which would prove whether or not they were witches. If they floated they were pulled out to be punished as witches; if they sank, they often drowned.

she is rightfully married, although it is not necessary. The Scotch church does not countenance these clandestine unions, and, I believe, excommunicates the contracting parties. The object of the laws of Scotland is, to prevent concubinage, by rendering it dangerous; not to facilitate improper marriages.

Nov. 27.—Dumbreck's hotel at Edinburgh is the most convenient, the quietest, the cheapest, and, at the same time, the most creditable of any establishment of this sort we have seen anywhere in Great Britain. Furnished lodgings are also very convenient. Two large sitting-rooms, and three bed-rooms, all on the first floor, decently furnished, may be had for four guineas a-week. The people of the house go to market, and cook for you. The table costs about a guinea a-day; a man-servant, three guineas and a half a-month. The distances in the new town are so little, that a carriage is quite unnecessary; sedan chairs are preferable, and very generally used. Hackney-coaches, besides, are here fit to be used by any body; and are on a much more decent footing in every respect than in London.

I regretted not having been present, during our residence in London, at some criminal trials; and, having mentioned it, I was obligingly invited to be present at one that took place yesterday in the Court of Justiciary, for a case of murder. At ten o'clock in the morning, we entered a handsome modern built hall. There was on one side a recess, and elevated seats for the judges, and before them, lower down, a table where the lord-advocate sat, with the counsel for the prisoner, and other lawyers. On one side, near the window, were the jury, on four benches, one behind the other, in an amphitheatre. Opposite to them, and fronting the light, a raised box for the witnesses. Fronting the judges, but outside of the bar, the prisoner sat between two soldiers; behind them, the public on an amphitheatre, reaching the very ceiling. The judges soon appeared, three in number. Their dress is very odd—gowns of red and white satin, stuck over with bows of red ribbon, and large wigs covering head and shoulders—a masquerade for which I was not prepared. Out of forty-five jurymen present, the presiding judge *selected* fifteen from a list he held in his hand, who were empanneled for the trial of the prisoner at the bar. This selection

Scotland

surprised me a little, I own. In England and in the United States the sheriff summons whom he pleases to serve on the jury. The names are put in a box, and twelve drawn out for every new trial. Here the sheriff summons likewise arbitrarily; but, instead of the jury being drawn by lot out of these, there is a second arbitrary selection by the judge—this is certainly doubly wrong. It seems to me, that all persons qualified to serve on the jury should be summoned successively in alphabetical order, and draw lots in court for each new pannel.

The accused has a right, here as well as in England, of challenging the jurymen—in this cause there was no challenge. After some previous formalities, the witnesses were produced, and examined in the absence of each other, which is much better than in England, and in the United States, where they are all allowed to be in hearing of each other. It appeared in evidence, that the prisoner and the deceased were neighbours, and that the former had been in the habit of passing with his cart through the yard of the latter. This privilege was disputed, and had given rise to many altercations. The prisoner coming one evening with his cart, found the passage obstructed by stones piled up for that purpose, and was removing the obstacle, when his adversary came forward to defend his entrenchment. In the course of the quarrel that ensued, the latter, (the dead man), struck the man with the cart, who, being much older, and very inferior in bodily strength, withdrew to his own house, and came back soon after, with a gun in his hand. Meanwhile, the wife of the deceased had drawn her husband away —he had left the yard, and was in his own garden, separated by a low hedge, when the prisoner advanced towards him, holding his gun forward, although not aiming. Most of the witnesses were workmen, who happened to be employed on the roof of a house at some distance; from that situation they had seen the prisoner approach the hedge which separated the parties, and they were very near each other when the gun went off, and the deceased fell. There was an attempt to show that the deceased had a stick in his hand, and struck the barrel of the gun just before it went off; but this part of the testimony coming from a boy, who seemed to have been instructed for that purpose, was not credited, and in fact injured the cause. The prisoner had been seen to move his arm, but whether he had touched the barrel was quite uncertain. On the other hand, nobody had seen him aim, or draw the trigger—the gun might have gone off by accident, and this bare possibility could alone save him. A great number of respectable witnesses vouched for the character of the prisoner, whose behaviour had always been irreproachable. The deceased bore, on the contrary, a very bad character—was a deserter—a poacher—bearing an assumed name, &c.; circumstances tending to establish, on one side, the improbability of the prisoner's intending anything more than to defend himself; and, on the other hand, the probability of the deceased being the aggressor in the quarrel. The testimony of the widow of the deceased, young, far gone in pregnancy, telling with great simplicity the tale of the murder of her husband in her presence, was a circumstance of fatal tendency. She could not, however, say any thing as to the immediate cause of the gun's going off, having turned away just then, with a child she had in her arms. After the Lord Advocate had established the proofs of the crime, and given his conclusions, the prisoner's counsel* rose, and making the best use of the weak and doubtful means the testimony afforded, spoke with great ingenuity—with clearness and acuteness, rather than pathetically, and without ambition of eloquence. The witnesses had all agreed that the prisoner, immediately after the fall of his adversary, had quietly set about removing the stone wall—a very singular circumstance, which had been adduced as a proof of the atrocity of his character, and as showing him capable of a premeditated murder; but from which his counsel inferred, with some appearance of reason, a consciousness of innocence, and that stupor, produced by a sudden and unforeseen accident, which had made him likewise unmindful of his own danger—for he did not fly, although not arrested till the next day, when he was found at home.

When the presiding judge charged the jury, which he did very ably, although, perhaps, with more energy than becomes the bench, I trembled for the prisoner. "This is murder or it is nothing," he said emphatically; "no medium."

* Francis Jeffrey Jeffrey (1773–1850). As well as being an advocate of great acuteness and insight, he was editor of the *Edinburgh Review*.

The jury, during all the stages of the trial, which lasted six hours, appeared to give the most meritorious attention; they were provided with pen and ink, and took notes. At four o'clock they withdrew to their chamber. The prisoner, clothed in black, decent, and resigned, listened to all that passed, without saying a word. He was soon after remanded to his prison, where, I presume, he did not spend a very comfortable night.

I have just learnt that the jury returned their verdict this morning, a majority of eleven to four deciding for *culpable homicide*, against the opinion of the bench, who wanted *no medium*. The judges passed the sentence of the law, which is transportation for life. The prisoner may have to wait two years in prison for a full cargo for Botany Bay.

The amusements and way of life in Edinburgh are, as may be supposed, as close an imitation of the customs and fashions of London, as relative circumstances of wealth, numbers, &c. can admit. There are here assemblies in the London style, made as numerous as possible; but, notwithstanding the efforts of a laudable emulation, the inhabitants of London being ten to one, Edinburgh routs cannot, by the nature of things, arrive at a perfection of crowds equal to those of the capital. It is often possible to sit and converse; cards, and even chess, are not quite excluded. You find generally one or two tables, with the pamphlets of the day, rare and valuable books carelessly heaped up, prints, drawings, and even children's play-things, which some are glad to take hold of, by way of appearing amused, when they are least disposed to be so. The piano is another play-thing, upon which a young and pretty hand is seen, but little listened to. I have observed that, in these numerous assemblies, music is the signal for a general *dechainement* of tongues; even those who were silent before, talk then, by the same sort of secret sympathy which swells the notes of the canary-bird in his cage to overpower conversation. A circle is formed round the instrument—people press about the performer, talking, *à qui mieux mieux*. It is indeed most true, nine times out of ten, the performer and her instrument produce at best but a harmonious noise—the more execution, the less music.

We could not be at Edinburgh without wishing to see the Caledonian bard, whose fertile and brilliant genius produces poems with the rapidity of thought—and we have been gratified. Mr Scott is a tall and stout man, thirty-five or forty years of age; very lame from some accident in his early youth.* His countenance is not particularly poetical—complexion fair, with a coarse skin—little beard—sandy hair—and light eyes and eye-brows—the *tout ensemble* rather dull and heavy: Yet when he speaks, which he is not always disposed to do, and is animated, his eye lightens up "With all a poet's extasy". This poet likes conviviality, and tells well, and *con amore*, such stories as are told here only after dinner. He is a great tory, and consequently a warm friend of liberty (in Spain)—a disposition, I have already observed, characteristic of his party.

Jan. 1. 1811.—There is no sleeping the first night of the year at Edinburgh. It is a received custom for the common people to give a kiss to any woman met in the streets, about midnight, on foot, or in carriages. Few women expose themselves to this rude salutation. But the streets are full, notwithstanding, of unruly boys, who knock at house doors, and make a noise all night. This is a little relic of the coarse manners of former times, which is still tolerated; and, considering what this country was before its union with England, there is, perhaps, more reason to be astonished at the advanced state of its police, than otherwise.

Jan. 14. 1811.—The winter has been felt severely in England; there has been much snow there, and the Thames has been frozen over; while here, in the latitude of Moscow, we have no snow; the grass is still green; the ground has scarcely been hard the whole winter, and skaiters have had but a few days amusement, on the piece of water at the foot of Arthur's Seat.

Jan. 25.—Dr T. having proposed to me to go to the anniversary dinner on Fox's birth-day; and wishing to see how these things are managed here, I went yesterday. The company was numerous; and the table filled a very large hall. Mr Gillies, an eminent advocate,

---

* Walter Scott (1771–1832) was, in fact, thirty-nine. The lameness was due to a feverish illness when he was a baby which left his right leg "much shrunk and contracted".

Scotland

presided.* The Honourable Henry Erskine, another celebrated lawyer, brother of Lord Erskine, chancellor during the ministry of Mr Fox, considered as the highest at the Scotch bar, assisted the president. After dinner several persons spoke successively. Among others, Mr E., in the simple tone of conversation. The necessity of a regency in the present state of the King's health; the hopes entertained from the political principles of the presumptive heir; parliamentary reform; emancipation of Ireland; and the other tenets of the party, were touched upon without violence; and the ministers themselves, notwithstanding the present crisis, were spoken of quite civilly. All party heat seemed to vent itself in mirth, *bon mots*, songs, and even puns—"tout comme chez nous." The whigs, indeed, believe they are on the eve of a great victory; and success puts people in good humour—in England, as elsewhere. I must mention one of the puns, not perhaps on account of its particular excellence, but to give an idea of the sort of thing, and of the easy, good-natured tone of the meeting. Mr N., a very good landscape painter, being cooped up in a corner, was obliged to jump over

---

* Adam Gillies (1760–1842). He became a lord of justiciary in 1812. Others mentioned in the ensuing account can be identified as Henry Erskine (1746–1817), at that time Lord Advocate of Scotland; the 8th Earl of Fingall (1759–1831), whose son, Arthur James, was at that time twenty and attending the university; James Murray, 8th Earl of Lauderdale (1759–1839), a shrewd but eccentric man—chief of the Whig party in Scotland and a strong opponent of the war with France—who had once, so it was said, appeared in Parliament "in the rough costume of Jacobinism". His son, Anthony, had fought in the Navy under Nelson. Mr N., the "very good landscape painter", is presumably Patrick Nasmyth who was born in Edinburgh in 1787, the son of Alexander Nasmyth (1758–1840) who might also be considered worthy of Simond's description. Lord N. can be more certainly identified as Charles Hay, Lord Newton, one of the senators of the College of Justice. He died nine months after this dinner in October 1811. He is described in William Forbes Gray's *Some old Scottish Judges* as "a zealous Whig when Toryism seemed to have gained a permanent ascendancy . . . an excessively corpulent man with lustrous eyes and a countenance as crimson as the robes he wore".

Dr T., who accompanied Simond to the dinner, is probably the Rev Dr Alexander Turnbull (1748–1831), a distant relative of Fox, a member of Lord Gillies's circle and a prominent figure in the Edinburgh "Whig Set". It was considered rather daring to attend a Fox anniversary dinner at this date, so no guest list survives.

the table to get out. Mr E. saw him, and the grave man of law called out, "Ah! N., this is one of your land-skips!" (landscapes.)

The name of Fox was, as of right, the first toast; then, very loyally, his Majesty; the seven unanimous brothers; the young Princess, brought up in the principles of Fox; the catholics of Ireland. On this last, Lord Fingall, a distinguished catholic of Ireland, now at Edinburgh for the education of his son, made an appropriate speech, modest, and, to appearance, unstudied. Lord Maitland merely thanked the company when Lord Lauderdale was given. Lord N., the only judge present, being named, I looked with some degree of anxiety at the learned lord, in appearance a true *porçeau d'epicure*, of a monstrous size—face of a blue raw colour—breathing hard—his eyes shut—he appeared stupified with good cheer, and ready to fall under the table; but the unwieldy mass soon stood up, and in a powerful, though broken and faltering voice, addressed the meeting in a short, moderate, sensible speech, hinting delicately at his being the only judge appointed by Mr Fox. Lord Erskine, and the trial by jury, was another of the toasts I remember.

When I left the house, about eleven at night, there was not the smallest appearance of intoxication; about one-third of the company had retired before me; the rest followed soon after, except, as I understood this morning, a knot of *bons vivants*, the big judge at their head, who did not separate till break of day, drinking all the time; and, what is most remarkable, this same judge was seen this morning going to Court, in as full possession of his faculties of body and mind as if he had spent the night in bed! This is a sample of the old northern manners. I had met this judge a few days before at a private dinner. The son of one of his old associates dining there also, was in mourning for his father. "Ah!" said the judge, "your father would not believe me; I told him he would kill himself; what! to reduce himself in his old age to a single bottle of wine at his dinner—it was certain death!" Lord N. I must do him the justice to say, has the reputation of being an excellent judge.

It is now fifteen years since the revolutionary impulse given by France was felt here with considerable violence. The heat is now subdued; not a spark of the fire remains alive; and the controversists of that time meet now very sociably, and seem to retain no remembrance of the mortal hatred they once bore to each other. I have been assured, that, in 1794, only thirteen persons durst meet to celebrate the anniversary dinner of Mr Fox, and the names of the thirteen patriots, taken down at the door, were sent to the high-handed minister of the day, as suspected persons. There were one hundred and fifty guests at this same celebration last year; yesterday, fifty more—this accession is suspected to be composed of that description of persons denominated rats; the little animals of that name having the instinctive sagacity of abandoning old buildings when they are going to fall down.

Feb. 1.—There has been a snow storm in the night, and it blows a hurricane; tiles fly across the streets, and tops of chimneys fall on the pavement, to the great annoyance of passengers, and danger of their lives. The house we inhabit, built of stone, is sensibly shaken by the wind. There is at the end of our street, on the mound, an itinerant menagerie built of boards; if it should be blown down, the people of Edinburgh might see at large in their streets two lions, two royal tigers, a panther, and an elephant, besides monkies, and other underlings of the savage tribe.

Feb. 6.—Bannister, an excellent English actor, is here.* We saw him yesterday in one of their wretched modern plays, *The Battle of Hexham*; the plot most absurd, and with a total want of taste; yet his inimitable acting covered all faults, and I was certainly much amused. He appeared also in *The Devil to Pay*—overcharged a good deal, but still excellent. The house was empty—not a single person in most of the boxes; and all this because of a concert where Braham sings†—a more fashionable amusement

---

* John Bannister (1760–1836). Formerly an art student he was a friend of Rowlandson and Gainsborough. He made his name in a farce of the Haymarket in 1778, and subsequently became one of the most celebrated comedians of the day.

† John Braham (1774–1856). In the words of Walter Scott, Braham was "a beast of an actor, but an angel of a singer". Extremely popular he made a fortune from his tenor voice and paid £26,000 for the building of the St James's Theatre.

than the theatre—which is deemed, all over Great Britain, rather a vulgar amusement; and so *their* theatre certainly is.

The following days we have again partaken of the pleasures of the vulgar—Bannister always animated, and full of his part. The last time he gave us *The Bold Stroke for a Wife*, a low and improbable play, although a little better than the modern ones. The great merit of Bannister in this was, the harlequin activity with which he shifted his dress half a dozen times, and assumed new and different characters; he was very much applauded, but pleased me less than usual.

Between the play and the farce the public often calls for some favourite song; Bannister treated us twice with these lyric pieces, in the genuine national taste. I do not suppose that any thing at all comparable is to be met with in any other country or language; the style is *unique*; and if it was possible to give any idea of it by a translation, the *étourdis* on the other side of the channel would hardly believe that these things could divert their sage neighbours so much, and make the thinking nation laugh so heartily.

I have already mentioned the extreme uncleanliness of the old town of Edinburgh. Cloacina has there no temples; every sort of filth is thrown out of window, just as in the old town of Marseilles. Passing through the narrow streets, morning and evening, you scarcely know where to tread, and your head is as much in danger as your feet; a certain cry of *gardy loo*, is the warning of anything coming down; a derivation, I am told, of *gardez l'eau*. Mr L. who was ambassador in Spain,* and resided there many years, told us that Madrid was formerly much in the same state as his "own romantic town" of Edinburgh. The filth continually thrown out of windows used to meet in the middle of the narrow streets of Madrid, forming a high ridge, which remained till a heavy rain washed it partly away, these streets being generally on a slope. The minister d'Aranda declared he would make Madrid from the dirtiest to the cleanest city in the world, and he succeeded.† He in-

---

* Robert (later Sir Robert) Liston (1742–1836) was Ambassador at Madrid from 1783 to 1788.

† Pedro Pablo Abarca y Bolea, Count of Aranda (1718–99) was prime minister of Spain from 1766 to 1773 and again in 1792.

troduced common-sewers, and a large pipe against the front, and from top to bottom of each house. The difficulties he had to encounter were great; and, among other objections, it was stated that the air of Madrid was naturally much too sharp, and that the effluvia of its immense dunghill was a necessary corrective, and, by softening that keenness, made it wholesome.

Feb. 14.—New depôts of prisoners of war are forming in the environs of Edinburgh, and detachments of these unfortunate people, transported by sea from the south of England to Leith, have arrived here; they are first lodged in the Castle. I had been informed, that a great number of them had been seen marching barefooted in the half-frozen mud. Wishing to ascertain the fact, and, if possible, to alleviate their sufferings, I procured an introduction to Colonel Maghee, commanding at the fort, who had the goodness to go with me among the prisoners. I found 3 or 400 men, nearly all seafaring-people, in a small court, surrounded with palisadoes, in front of that part of the building where they lodge at night; this esplanade, about 100 or 120 feet every way, had a very beautiful view of the town and country over the brow of the hill. I do not suppose, however, these unfortunate people were much disposed to enjoy it. I found them walking to and fro in their narrow inclosure, most of them talking merrily enough, poorly clad, although not in rags. Those who have no clothes of their own receive certain yellow jackets, which, by their remarkable appearance, render an escape more difficult; instead of shoes, they had most of them a sort of galoches, the sole of wood and top of list. I understood that many had lost their shoes in the muddy road, and that 150 of them were really in great want of that important article, which Colonel Maghee assured me was to be supplied before they left the castle to go to the depôt. The daily ration is $1\frac{1}{2}$lb. bread at 3d.; $\frac{1}{2}$lb. of meat at $6\frac{3}{4}$d. per lb.; once or twice a week they have fish instead of meat; each man is provided with a hammock and two blankets. Many supplicating hands offered for sale the produce of their industry; watch-chains made of hair, and other trifling articles, most of them very ingeniously manufactured. A young man, his countenance all radiant with good-humour, informed me he had been seven years thus encaged, having been one of the first taken at the renewal of the war. If he is proof against such a fate as this, he need not envy any one. The richest gifts of fortune are poor indeed, compared to an indestructible power of happiness.

I observed, on the other hand, several prisoners traversing slowly, apart from the rest, the narrow and muddy area, or leaning back against the paling, with sunken eyes, fixed and dull looks, and earthy complexions—wrapt in meditation upon nothing. It is shocking to think that fifty or sixty thousand human beings should be in this deplorable situation! Not so many, however, feel it. The abject crowd was seen here pressing with eagerness and loud clamour—all speaking at the same time—round a spot where some game was going on, with the same bursts of laughter, the same oaths and frantic gestures, as if their dearest interests had been in question. An aristocrat *à la lanterne*, the execution of Robespierre, or the news of a cartel for the general exchange of prisoners, could not have excited more bustle and agitation! This is the best possible school for idleness and vice, as well as an abode of unspeakable wretchedness, to all those whose feelings are not blunted. If the persons on whom the liberation of so many miserable men depends could be placed for a little while in the midst of them, it is scarcely possible to suppose that the negociation for the exchange should not be facilitated thereby. Many of the prisoners seemed too old to be worth keeping, and might be sent back without any accession of strength to the enemy. I have heard of an East India captain, who was taken in 1793, liberated in 1802; taken again the following year, and now a prisoner with a wife and family in France!

Officers are allowed their parole, and receive 1s. 6d. a day from the British government for their support; the common men, either soldiers or sailors, cost about 10d. exclusive of houses and other contingent expences; 1s. sterling a head is probably the lowest computation—which, for 50,000 prisoners, is L. 2500 per day, or nearly one million a-year, besides the expence of the troops necessary to guard this army of prisoners. An exchange on any terms would be better than this. I cannot help thinking that some useful employment might be found for these men, such as roads and canals, or the tillage of waste lands.

A woman died in the upper story of the house in which we lodge, rather poor, and but little addicted during her life to the luxury of a carriage; but it has been made up to her at last, and she has just taken her departure from the door in a coach and six, covered with black cloth, and surmounted with plumes of feathers of the same colour, followed by more carriages, with a number of hired mourners on foot, before and behind, in black, and carrying likewise black plumes of feathers. You meet these processions of funeral vehicles every day, here and in England, on the high roads, and in the crowded streets of great cities. Their solemnity forms, at the same time, a sad and ridiculous contrast with the light and rapid motion of the carriages of the living, splashing them as they drive by, and the indifference of the passing throng, who heed not this last effort of the vanity of man, and hurry on without bestowing a single look on the show. Some of the friends of the deceased follow in the carriages. The lower people bury their dead on foot, and the nearest relatives walk in the train. A husband follows the body of his wife—a wife of her husband— parents their children—and the lover his mistress. This custom is still kept up in the largest cities of the United States, as well as in the country. It is making grief a show, or indifference a scandal, and violating the sacredness of feeling.

Some persons of rank have come here lately on purpose to effect very odd transfers of matrimonial partners.* Lady Charlotte W. had the misfortune of falling violently in love with Lord P., who has the reputation of being irresistible in love as well as in war,

* The people involved in this notorious case were Lady Charlotte Wellesley, wife of Henry Wellesley (a younger brother of the Duke of Wellington) and daughter of the 1st Earl Cadogan; Lord Paget, the cavalry commander who, as Lord Uxbridge, was to lose a leg at Waterloo and, five days after the battle, to be created Marquess of Anglesey; the 6th Duke of Argyll; and Lady Paget, formerly Lary Caroline Elizabeth Villiers, daughter of the Earl of Jersey.

Having obtained the necessary divorces, Lord Paget—the father, as Simond says, of six children—married Lady Charlotte Wellesley by whom he had ten more children, and the Duke of Argyll married Lady Paget. The Duke and Duchess had no children and the Dukedom passed to his brother.

and ran away with him. The husband of this lady, who is a reasonable man, offered to receive her again if she would come back before the step she had taken became public; but she chose to be constant in her inconstancy, and finally a divorce was the consequence. It is not the fashion to fight for a wife it seems, but only for a sister; the brother of Lady C. W. challenged the gallant, who, with true delicacy of honour, and the confidence of a man whose courage could not be doubted, avoided, as long as he could, placing himself in a situation where he might have to shed the blood of the brother, after having dishonoured the sister. This couple are come to Scotland to be married. There were, however, difficulties in the way, Lord P. being already a married man; but as infidelity on the male side is a legitimate cause of divorce in Scotland, he took care to furnish his wife with the plea. She might have played her rival the trick of not suing for a divorce; but love furnished a remedy to the evils he had caused—and the Duke of A. intervening, *bien-à-propos*, persuaded the forsaken lady to part with her husband, and become a duchess. The parties, therefore, changing sides, Lady C. W. has married Lord P., and Lady P. the Duke of A. The former is said to have lost by this arrangement an amiable and a handsome woman, for one who wants one at least of these advantages; a wife he loved, for another he does not care about; without any apparent motive except pure *devouement*. It is remarkable enough, that one of these new couples has already a family of fourteen children; the present Lady P. having had eight before her divorce, and Lord P. six.

Feb. 20.—Great complaints of commercial distress felt all over the kingdom, but particularly in the manufacturing towns, have reached even this place, which is so independent of trade; and the despondency about public affairs is visible. Among the many failures of which we hear every day, I was much surprised to find there were some farmers; one gentleman only has thirteen of his tenants bankrupts! Now the bankruptcy of a farmer would appear in France just as ridiculous as the bankruptcy of an apple-woman or a chimney-sweeper; but an English farmer, as I have remarked before, is properly a great manufacturer, and not a peasant; he is a man of business, who has his books regularly kept, and makes his payments on the appointed day. I did not know till lately that he has his banker also, who enables him to pay with this punctuality, by making occasional advances, on his personal responsibility, on the notes of the person to whom he has sold his produce, or on that produce itself, reserved for a better market. The advantages resulting to trade from these banking facilities are no less evident in regard to agriculture than to trade, but equally liable to abuses and inconveniences. The present distresses have occasioned several forced sales of lands, at low prices. An estate of 620 acres, between Glasgow and Edinburgh, with a vein of coal estimated at L. 6000, the buildings not in very good order, has just been sold for L. 35,000; in prosperous times it was estimated at L. 57,000.

After a residence of three months, we are going to leave Edinburgh, with feelings of regret and gratitude for the many marks of good-will and kindness we have received. Taken altogether, I do not know any town where it would be pleasanter to live. It is, in a great degree, the Geneva of Britain.

5

THE NORTH AND THE MIDLANDS
27 February 1811 – 24 March 1811

Feb. 27.—We are come to Alnwick, 29 miles from Berwick, the greatest part of the way in view of the sea, still glassy and blue, and dotted over with white sails. Farms in the best possible order, and on a great scale; immense stacks of hay and straw, and outhouses without number. Windmills also innumerable, for grain and for oil; most of the large farms have one. Each of these mills has a small windmill, or rather wind wheel, behind, to work the cap round to the wind; and not as in France, by means of a long lever, or tail, moved round by the miller to suit the wind. Some of the mills are so constructed, as to reef their sails by the mere force of the wind, when it reaches a certain strength, or feather their arms of themselves.

The hay or straw stacks, sliced down all round during the winter, are now reduced to the appearance of polygonal towers or pillars, 30 or 40 feet high, which still resist the wind and rain very well. These slices are cut with surprising neatness, from top to bottom of the stack, thatched roof and all, by means of a very sharp instrument.

The first appearance of the castle of Alnwick is certainly very striking, and yet ridiculous. Its walls are defended by a garrison of stone figures, shewing themselves between the battlements in threatening attitudes; some of them armed cap-a-pee—others stark naked, recruited indifferently from antiquity and from modern times. Hercules brandishes his club, and Apollo shoots his arrows, while British crossbow-men, arquebusiers, level their pieces at the assailants, and menials throw stones. We shall visit this puppet-show castle tomorrow, more at leisure.

Feb. 28.—We went to the castle early this morning; the apartments not visible on account of the recent birth of a grand-daughter of the Duke of Northumberland's. They must be dull, surrounded as they are by high walls, and the view from the windows being confined to a court-yard. The chapel is highly gilt, and gaudily ornamented; the pedigree of the Percys is inscribed on its walls, beginning by Charlemagne, 800, the Conqueror, 1060, &c. A place of Christian worship seems the most unfit imaginable for this display of worldly greatness. Not far from the gay chapel are the dungeons, with their grated trap-doors and loop-holes. In a recess of the wall we observed a wheel with iron teeth and a chain, and shuddered at the sight of what we took for an instrument of torture!—on inquiry, however, it turned out to be only an appendage of the dinner-bell. Some of the stone figures already mentioned are corroded by long exposure to the air, and worn to half their original size, while others appear quite whole and fresh. This led to the discovery, that this apparently old castle was in fact built only sixty years ago, but on the exact model of the old castle.* Such of the old figures as could at all stand on their legs returned to their former station on the walls, while the others were made new from the chisel of an eminent stone-cutter of the neighbourhood. The Percys of the eighteenth century seem to have been bent upon shewing that they had not degenerated from those of the ninth in point of taste in the fine arts. The park and grounds were laid out by *one Brown*, as the gardener told us; they are traversed by a stream of water, magnified into a river by being dammed up; a magnificent bridge is thrown over it. The ground slopes to the river on both sides, and is covered with the usual green carpeting of smooth turf, and sprinkled over with clumps of trees, which are small, and make no great figure. The Duke of Northumberland's landed estate is said to yield the prodigious income of L. 150,000 sterling a-year.

From Alnwick to Newcastle, 33 miles; a continuation of the same rich, well-cultivated country, but bare of trees, and without any beauty. The inhabitants strike us as better looking than in Scotland; the women certainly are handsomer; the men have smaller features—are more plump and rosy than the Scotch. The houses are much cleaner. The children we meet on the road stop

* Alnwick Castle was later restored by Anthony Salvin (1799–1881). The *"one Brown"* to whom the gardener refers is, of course, Lancelot "Capability" Brown (1715–83).

and make a bow, which is not the custom in Scotland. The whin also, of which the roads are still composed, is broken in smaller pieces—everything thus bearing the marks of more advanced civilization.

March 1.—The name of Newcastle is identified with that of coals, the country about containing immense strata of this mineral, which is the object of a great trade. There are farms under ground as well as on the surface, and leased separately. I know of a subterranean farm of this kind of 5000 acres, for which L. 3000 sterling a-year is paid, and a per centage depending on the quantity of coals extracted, which may double that rent.

I accepted with pleasure an invitation to descend in a coalmine. The mode is rather alarming. The extremity of the rope which works up and down the shaft being formed into a loop, you pass one leg through it, so as to sit, or to be almost astride on the rope; then, hugging it with both arms, you are turned off from the platform over a dark abyss, where you would hardly venture if the depth was seen. This was 63 fathoms deep (378 feet). One of the workmen bestrode the loop by the side of me, and down we went with considerable rapidity. The wall of rock seemed to rush upwards—the darkness increased—the mouth above appeared a mere speck of light. I shut my eyes for fear of growing giddy; the motion soon diminished, and we touched the ground. Here we stopped for two other persons. Each of us had a flannel dress and a candle, and thus proceeded through a long passage—rock above, rock below—and a shining black wall of coal on each side; a railway in the middle for horses (for there are fifty or sixty horses living in this subterraneous world), to draw two four-wheel carriages, with each eight large baskets of coal; these baskets are brought one at a time by diminutive waggons, on four little wheels, drawn or pushed by boys along other rail-ways, coming down the side streets to this main horse-road, the ceiling of which is cut in the main rock, high enough for a man to stand upright, while the side streets are no higher than the stratum of coals ($4\frac{1}{2}$ feet), therefore you must walk stooping.

The whole extent of the mine is worked in streets, intersecting each other at right angles, 24 feet wide and 36 feet asunder, leaving therefore solid blocks 36 feet every way. The miners have two enemies to contend with, air and water; that air is hydrogen gas, continually emitted by the coals, with an audible hissing noise. The contact of the lights necessary to be used would infallibly set fire to the hydrogen gas, if allowed to accumulate, and either blow up or singe the miners severely; it is therefore necessary that there should be a continual current of air going in and out by two different issues. At the beginning of the works, and while there is only one shaft, this is effected by means of a wooden partition, carried down along the middle of the shaft, then along the first street opened, and so disposed afterwards, that the air which comes down the shaft on one side of the partition, may circulate successively through each and every street before it returns up the other division of the shaft, a small fire establishing and keeping up the draught. As to water, the dip, or inclination of the stratum of coals being known, all the art consists in making the first shaft in the lowest part of the tract; a steam-engine at the top drains up the water, and draws up the coals. Wherever the shaft comes in contact with any stratum yielding water, it must be kept out by means of a drum, or lining of timber, made tight round the inside of the shaft. I saw a small spring of clear water issuing from the bed of coal below, near the stables where the horses are kept, and serving to water them. These horses are in very good order; their coats soft and glossy, like the skin of a mole: they are conveyed down, or taken out, with great care and expedition, by means of a great net or bag.

Some of the mines are more extensive than the city of Philadelphia, and their streets are as regular. When the whole area is thus excavated in streets, it must not be supposed that the solid blocks are abandoned; but, beginning at the furthest extremity, the miners proceed to pull down all the blocks one after the other. When a space of two or three hundred feet square has been thus left unsupported, the ceiling of solid rock begins to sag and crack, with a hideous noise; the workmen go on notwithstanding, trusting that the ceiling will not break down close to the blocks, but some way behind; and such is the case—the cracks grow wider and wider—the rock bends down, coming at last in contact with the floor—and the whole extent is thus filled up. On the surface of the ground, however, nothing is perceived; the rocks are left to manage the business among themselves below. Houses—and stone houses too—remain standing, and their inhabitants sleep in peace all the while.

The miners know, by the nature of the rocks they meet while sinking the shaft, when they approach the coal, which is generally found between two beds of white sandstone. They sink the shaft at the rate of about two fathoms a-week.

The consumption of London has increased one-fourth in the course of the last few years; it amounts now to about 1,000,000 chaldrons, or 1,200,000 tons annually, forming 6000 cargoes of vessels of 200 tons each; and as they perform twelve voyages a-year, the trade employs 500 ships; the crews consist of two old sailors, for captain and mate, and seven or eight apprentices, all protected from impressment; the two old men have L. 9 each voyage. The mere coal trade between Newcastle and London is, therefore, a nursery for 4000 young sailors, and a preferment for 1000 old ones. The celebrated navigator, Captain Cook, had served his time on board a collier.

The coal drawn to the surface of the soil is conveyed to the lighters by means of low carriages, on four small wheels fixed to their axis, that their motion may be perfectly equal. They travel on rail-ways, which are composed of two bars of iron, upon which the wheels, which have grooves at their circumference, run without impediment. Ninety-two bushels, weighing about two tons, besides the waggon, are drawn by a single horse, with so much ease, that the driver is obliged, on the least descent of the road, to press on the wheel with a sort of lever, to retard its motion by the friction, that the carriage may not run too much on the horse. The lighters, called keels, of about fifteen tons, carry the coals on board vessels waiting in deep water. It is remarked, that the men employed under ground enjoy better health than those on the surface; the regularity of temperature securing them against many disorders, and the air constantly renewed being sufficiently pure.

March 5.—York, by Newby Hall, 28 miles. Newby Hall is one of those innumerable fine houses, scattered over this country, which are allowed to be shewn to strangers. This one, however, is distinguished from the crowd, by a collection of antique marbles of much reputation. Mr W. the last proprietor, took the trouble of collecting himself abroad, at a vast expence, these remains of Grecian art.* His Venus alone, we were told, cost L. 15,000 sterling; a great price, undoubtedly; but the satire of Voltaire will not apply here, for although *acheté cher,* this is not a *moderne antique.*

York is an old town, and of course very ugly, containing about 15,000 inhabitants. Its Minster is one of the wonders of England, 50 feet longer than Westminster Abbey, which is, I think, 520 [513] feet. The main tower over the centre is heavy; the two lesser ones are much better; the rest of the exterior is light and beautiful. The interior is very striking indeed, and superior to any thing we have yet seen, as to boldness, lightness, and prodigious high finish of the carving—quite sharp and *à jour.* The figures introduced are in the usual barbarous grotesque style. The outside carving, originally as highly finished, having been much injured by time, is now undergoing thorough repairs, or rather an entire new facing; the modern carving is fully equal to the old, and made like in colour by oiling the stones. Beautiful as the inside of the Minster undoubtedly is, I think it less striking than the inside of St Paul's; the latter is something less in size, but its vast airy dome, and the wide area under it, produce a greater effect. The tower of a small Gothic church near the Minster is remarkable light and beautiful. The windows of the Minster are too large, and admit too much light.

On Sunday the judges, just arrived for the assizes, came to church *en grand costume,* with their huge powdered wigs, and black robes; but all their smartness was lost upon us, who had just seen the Scotch judges dressed in white and pink satin. The mayor and corporation swelled the train, and in the rear footmen in white liveries, and large nosegays at the button-hole; the whole town was in motion. The assizes in a country town are an event;

* Newby Hall, one of the country's finest Adam houses, still contains its extensive collection of classical statuary, collected by William Weddell (1725-92).

The North and the Midlands

and it puts me in mind of Mad. de Stael's witty remark, "On ne s'y amuse une fois, que pour découvrir que l'on s'y ennuie tous les jours." The chanting was very good, and the voices of some of the young choristers admirable, but the organist flourished too much.

We had the pleasure of seeing here the Rev. S. S. who has been the delight of the devout fashionables of the capital; it is not, however, in this character we have known him, but in his own house, where, among his friends, he is a most agreeable companion. He has the reputation of being one of the most lively writers of the Edinburgh Review, and serious too, when he pleases. His countenance struck me as very like that of the unfortunate Louis XVI, with more vivacity in the eye.*

There is near York a retreat for lunatics, which appears admirably managed, and almost entirely by *reason* and kindness; it was instituted by the Quakers. Most of the patients move about at liberty, without noise and disorder, and by their demure and grave deportment shew they have not quite forgotten to what sect they belong. We observed, however, in a great garden or court, some men in broad brim hats, walking about in a hurried agitated manner, with their hands in their coat-pockets, where we found at last they were confined. The lowest only of the patients are allowed to be seen; for the Quakers recognize in practice some inequalities of rank. It is impossible, however, to blame those who wish not to expose the infirmities of their friends to the idle gaze of the curious. The mistress of the house is a good-looking, portly lady, lately married to the keeper, both Quakers. You cannot say of this couple, with Molière, "Du coté de la barbe est toute la puissance;" for all the consequence and the talents seem here on the side of the lady, and her husband appears merely her deputy. The frame of the windows is of iron, which saves the appearance of grates. Some of the patients are allowed to go out of the premises, and even to town alone. The directress told us that, having been indisposed in consequence of a fall, and some little dispute having arisen some time afterwards with one of the female

---

* The Rev Sydney Smith (1771–1845). Since 1809 he had been living in exile from the fashionable world in the isolated parish of Foston-le-Clay.

patients, the latter said to her, "I am sorry to see that since thy fall thee hast not been quite *right*, and if it should last we shall be obliged to take care of thee!" We heard some other curious traits; I shall mention only the following. A young and stout female patient, displeased with one of the servants, threw her down on the floor, and holding her there said, "What should hinder me from strangling thee? I am mad; they could not hang me for it!"

In fourteen years 154 patients have been admitted; of which 73 have been cured, 24 have died (three by suicide), and 57 remain. There are more women than men. The most ordinary causes are love, religion, pride, and reverses in fortune; two of these causes apply more particularly to the sex—the other two are equally divided. I have been told by a well-informed person, born a Quaker, that there are more instances of insanity among that persuasion than among other people; the rich particularly are most exposed to this calamity. Commerce and manufactures are nearly the only professions from which Quakers do not exclude themselves; but the sons of rich merchants, caring little about trade, and almost all kinds of amusements, the fine arts, and certain departments of literature, falling under the same interdiction, nothing remains but *ennui*, nervousness, and at last insanity.

The Rev. Sydney Smith who had the goodness to accompany us, said he had understood there was an undue proportion of tailors among mad people. I would not answer that this remark was to be taken seriously.

Madness appears to be fatally common in Great Britain, and among the higher ranks, as well as among quakers and tailors. I have heard of three families of Scotch dukes, in which there have been, from time to time, cases of this kind, and eleven earls' families. My informant, who was not so well acquainted with the state of noble brains in the southern section of the island, could not name more than three families of mad English dukes; and the case of an illustrious personage belongs by blood rather to Scotland than to England: Yet the Scotch talk of this calamity as afflicting peculiarly England—seeing the mote in their brother's eye and not the beam in their own.

March 11.—We are just returned from Castle Howard. Traversing York this morning, in our way there, we met the judges going to open the sessions, with the same wigs and the same train as yesterday. The whole town was in motion—the streets full of misses in white muslin—citizens in dark blue coats, carefully brushed, glossy hats, and shining boots—and military people in red. It seemed a day of rejoicing; and in fact the whole time of the sessions is a period of amusement; yet we learn that the prisons here are unusually full. There are eight cases of murder, and among them a young couple for beating their own child, an infant, to death. One might be disposed to judge unfavourably, at first sight, of people who take this time for rejoicing; but the extraordinary concourse of people, and not their purpose, is the occasion of it. The English think very highly of their own humanity; I am willing to admit they are not inhuman, although their history is undoubtedly very sanguinary. More blood has been spilt here by the sword of the law than anywhere else—in France by the hands of the mob, or mob tribunals. There is nothing in the English history to match the French St Barthélemy, or the late phrenetic period of revolution. But England, in times of good order, and regular government, was in the habit of shedding on the scaffold, reign after reign, the blood of her noblest and most illustrious citizens. The French have shown, perhaps, more genuine ferocity, the English a hardier and more inexorable character.

March 12.—We took leave of our friends after dinner, and are settled at Leeds for the night, 22 miles, through a rich and highly cultivated country, farm-houses in sight everywhere, with their usual appendages, in great order, and the polygonal pillars of hay already mentioned. Large fields fresh ploughed, black and smooth, others ploughing, always with horses, never with oxen. Farmers riding among their workmen—great flocks of sheep confined by net-fences in turnip fields. The meadows are of the most vivid green, and the trees are budding, much as about New York a month later—the weather so fine and mild as to travel with the glasses down. Stage-coaches pass us continually with their absurd lading of passengers on the top—twelve or fifteen nodding heads. The night had closed when we approached Leeds, and from a height, north of the town, we saw a multitude of fires issuing, no doubt from furnaces, and constellations of illuminated windows (manufactories) spread over the dark plain. We soon reached streets of good-looking shops, and stopped at the door of the inn— a large bustling one, always less comfortable than those of lesser towns.

The clothiers' hall is a vast quadrangular fire-proof building round a court-yard; it is the joint property and warehouse of 2000 private manufacturers, half-farmers, who have only a loom or two kept going at leisure times. Twice a-week, for one hour, they appear each at his stand, two and a half feet wide, and perhaps ten feet deep, with their stock piled up behind them, and samples in their hands. These stands are arranged on each side of a long gallery, with a passage between.

The merchants walk along the double line comparing their orders with the samples, and making purchases, generally at a uniform price. There is a great deal of business done in a very short time, and with very few words, although many of the stands are occupied by women, as our conductress informed us. This is a respectable set of people, and a pleasing instance of domestic manufactures, so preferable to the crowds and depravity of great establishments. Cloth has lately fallen in price from 33 to 25 shillings, in consequence of the increasing obstructions to the British trade.

The men, whose business is the combing and shearing the cloth, work by the piece, and earn 5s. a-day, by working from four in the morning to eight at night. They are described as very extravagant and very poor; brutified, vicious, and troublesome to their employers. They see, with an evil eye, a machine about to be set up, to do this work by the steam-engine, and disturbances are apprehended. We have observed the mark of *Joumaux frères, de Sedan*, on pieces of broad-cloth destined for the continent.

The hospital, or infirmary, is remarkable for the good order and cleanliness of its interior; the patients are placed in rooms, not wards, from four to eight in each. The only improvement the philanthropic Howard, visiting this hospital, could suggest, was that there ought to be a sufficient number of apartments for some

John Burke fights Tom O'Connell

Bootham Bar, York

Temple Row West and Colmore Row, Birmingham

Piccadilly: the Egyptian Hall

Gateway at Newgate

Hackney in Simond's time

The North and the Midlands

of them in rotation to remain unoccupied for some weeks, which was done accordingly.

This town has doubled in the last twenty years, therefore a great part of the buildings are modern and comfortable, with gardens, planted squares, and flowers in every window. We were shown a good library and reading-room; the librarian is a lady.

We left Leeds late in the day, and, in consequence of a scarcity of horses on the road, we could not proceed farther than Barnsley (twenty miles); and here we are in the worst inn which we have met with in this country.

March 14.—Sheffield is another steam-engine town, all iron, and steel, and smoke, but we shall see enough of all this at Birmingham. These Cyclops, however, have very pretty country-houses, all fresh and green, round their smoky workshop—mostly on the slope of a hill, from which the view is very extensive, over a rich and fertile country.

On approaching Castleton, our quarters for the night, the very old castle, from which it derives its name, appears behind, on the brow of a high perpendicular rock. It was a ruin at the time of the Romans, who called it *Arx Diaboli*, and its origin was then unknown. With a guide, who introduced himself on our arrival, we proceeded immediately to the renowned cavern, called the Peak's Hole, at the foot of the rock of the castle. I was struck, on approaching it, with its resemblance to the rock of the *fontaine de Vaucluse*. The entrance is 120 feet wide, and 70 feet high. Advancing under the spacious dome, we were surprised to see several small houses lost in its immensity, and a number of twine-makers, who have been in possession of this work-shop time immemorial. Here we received each of us a lighted candle, and, descending by a narrow passage at the extremity of the first cavern, we soon came to a little lake of very clear water, covering the area of a second cavern, the ceiling of which was so low, that, crossing the water in a boat, you are obliged to lie down. On landing on the other side, we found ourselves in the third division of this subterranean suite of apartments. This one, still more vast than the first, is 250 feet square, and 120 feet high. The guides, who understand their business, prepare here a little *coup-de-théâtre* for the curious under their protection. Some children, brought up to the part they are to act, reach the spot before-hand, and, ascending a sort of natural circular gallery at a great height, place themselves in picturesque attitudes, with lights in their hands, and sing. The effect produced by these angels of darkness is undoubtedly very striking. You next come to a long passage, and a slippery descent of 150 feet, so low that you cannot stand upright without danger for your head against sharp inequalities of the rock; and, however fatal a place of this sort may be to the lustre of a new hat, I would not advise any body to leave it at the entrance of the cavern, as I had done. You meet here with a stream of water flowing rapidly along, which must be crossed several times by means of stepping-stones, or upon the ready back of the guide. The stream soon finds its way through a side-opening in the rock, where it is lost. At last, after a toilsome journey of perhaps half a mile, you reach nearly the farthest extremity of the cavern, and must make haste to turn back before the candles are burnt out, which would leave you in a distressed plight. The children and their lights surprise you again on your return in a new and beautiful situation; but the most striking part of the whole is the distant reappearance of day-light illuminating the arch of the great entrance. The whole interior cavern is at times full of water. An internal stream rushes out of the rock, and in again at another place, but never reaches the great entrance. After the waters have subsided, stones are found of a nature totally different from the surrounding rock, as well as plants and sticks. The body of a snake, or some long shaped fish, is shown in the rock, which is calcareous.

After a hasty dinner, we set out again with our guide for another subterraneous expedition, bent upon fulfilling the utmost of our duties as tourists. The night was beautiful, clear, starry, and cool, and the hills illuminated with fires of furze and broom.

At the entrance of the Speedwell lead-mine, we were provided each with a candle, and descended 106 slippery steps in the rock; at the bottom of which we found a boat, and embarked on a subterranean canal seven feet wide, filling a horizontal gallery wholly cut in the rock, with about two feet of water. The long narrow boat glided along swiftly, impelled by the men giving a shove now and then against the rock on either side. A noise, as of a distant cataract, soon attracted our attention, and, increasing every moment, would certainly have occasioned great terror, if we had not been confident that our conductors knew what they were about. At last, when the noise was at the loudest, we emerged suddenly from the narrow gallery into open space and darkness; a cavern of immeasurable height above, and, close to us on the left, an abyss, into which the water of our canal, and a pretty considerable stream, coming from higher parts of the cavern, fell over a low stone wall, which alone prevented our boat from sliding in. It was rather a frightful sight. One of the miners, climbing up the rocks on the right a good way with some dry wood, provided for the purpose, lighted a fire, which discovered to us vast recesses; but there was still a space above which reflected no light. Sky-rockets have been sent up in the vast void without meeting the top. Miners have been let down the water-fall by a rope, and found, at 90 feet depth, an immense reservoir, into which they threw the lead, which touched only at 300 feet. An old miner who was in the boat, told us of their surprise and terror, when, after years of labour (five or six years, I think) and, piercing about 900 yards into the rock in search of veins of lead, of which they found now and then specimens, they broke suddenly into this great cavern, and heard the tremendous rushing of water. They soon, however, not only familiarized themselves with the cataract, but thought of profiting by it; and building the low wall already mentioned, across the very brink of the fall, threw two feet of water in their gallery, which made it navigable. They then began another gallery in a line with the first, on the other side of the cavern. Five or six years more, and a progress of another half mile, brought them to a second cavern, not so high or deep as the first, but extending infinitely further. They explored it for three miles without finding the extremity. The area is very rugged and irregular, and there is no knowing exactly where it ends. But there is a sensible current of air through it; the flame of candles pointing always to one side, and burning bright, and the respiration of men quite free. All the stones and rubbish of the second gallery were thrown into the waterfall without any perceivable diminution of depth. The whole work lasted eleven years. No vein sufficiently rich to pay the expence was discovered; but it will remain a lasting monument of industry and perseverance, though unhappily not rewarded; and afford a curious insight into the interior state of calcareous rocks, which seem all to be more or less intersected with such immense caverns, and reservoirs of springs and rivers. Beautiful crystals of carbonate of lime, known by the name of Derbyshire spar, and remains of fish and plants, are discovered every day in excavating the mines of this neighbourhood. There are several other level galleries in Derbyshire longer than that of the Speedwell mine—one is four miles long. On our return, one of our miners, a dwarfish old man, regaled us with a song, *"Black-ey'd Susan,"* in a voice of thunder, as little harmonious as it was powerful.

March 15.—Our first stage this morning was Chatsworth. The road, on leaving Castleton, ascends for half an hour, affording fine views. Pounded marble and calcareous spar sparkled everywhere in the sun. It is the finest weather imaginable—not a cloud in the horizon.

We observed a number of men peeling off the surface of a heath by the laborious process described before, burning it in heaps, and scattering the ashes. This does not answer, we are told, for peat land, which requires lime.

From the inn at Chatsworth, we walked across the park to the house, which is extremely handsome and palace-like, more so indeed than any house we have seen in England, although not so large as some others. It is built half way up a sloping lawn, terminated at the bottom by a very pretty lively stream, and above, behind the house, by lofty woods. Fine single trees dispersed over the lawn; a good-looking stone-bridge over the river.

The domestics of these noble houses are generally as obsequious as inn-keepers, and from the same motives. Porters, footmen, gardeners, waited upon us immediately. The apartments have nothing remarkable; gobelin tapestry, old, faded, and in wretched taste; and numerous pictures still worse. It is quite inconceivable that a person of so cultivated a taste as the last Duchess should have been able to bear the sight of these daubs. We hear,

The North and the Midlands

indeed, that for many years she did not come here. The household seemed to have great hopes from their young master, who, the gardener informed us, cares more about the beauties of the place than his father.*

Our second stage has been Matlock, (28 miles to-day;) the country varied, cultivated like a garden, and covered with gentlemen's houses; elegant cottages and farm-houses; spires and towers of small Gothic churches, some of them very beautiful, peeping over groves of trees:—The general appearance of things certainly much superior to that of Scotland. There are poor people here undoubtedly at 2s. 6d. a-day; and the 4s. or 5s. in the pound of the poor's rates are not paid for nothing; yet, I do not know how it is, these poor are not seen; and if it was not for the usual threatening notices at the entrance of towns and villages against *"vagrants found loitering,"* &c. a traveller would not suspect there were such persons. The expedient the great Frederick had adopted, to prevent dragoons falling from their horses, is well known; he had them flogged. And "certain it is," an officer said to Dr Moore, "they no longer fall." Perhaps the fear of overseers prevents the English falling into poverty.

We see, with regret, the finest hedge-row trees falling under the axe everywhere, and yet, if it had not been for the use made of them, they never would have been planted. There is still a sufficient number remaining to give the country that woody appearance peculiar to English landscape. A large piece of timber is a mine; and, in order to dispose of it to the best advantage, a temporary shed is sometimes erected by it, particularly if it is an ash, to work it on the spot into pieces fitted for various purposes, calculating and combining so exactly, as to waste nothing.

The vale of Matlock is renowned for its beauty. It presents, on the opposite side of a boisterous stream, vertical cliffs of calcareous rocks, worn, broken, and cavernous, edged with trees above and below. Several mineral springs flow down to the river; and this is

* This young master, William, 6th Duke of Devonshire (1790–1858) succeeded to the title in 1811. It was he who was responsible for employing Jeffrey Wyatville to remodel and extend the house and who employed Joseph Paxton as gardener.

one of the places of general resort for people who want to be cured, or for those who want to be amused; but this is not the season; it is empty, and we have our choice of hotels. The one where we are has a tepid bath, or at least not quite cold, 20 feet wide, 40 feet long, and four feet deep, incessantly renewed by a natural spring bubbling up in the middle; the temperature of which is always 68° or 69° of Fahrenheit, and perfectly clear and pure.

We have seen several goitres, although not large, since we entered Derbyshire—we did not observe any in the Highlands of Scotland.

March 19.—At Birmingham, where we have been two days, we have been employed in seeing wonders of ingenuity and skill applied to the most trifling, as well as to the most important objects, with a merchant of this place, who was so obliging as to be our guide. The manufactories are mostly of hardware and glass, and are less unhealthy, although more dirty, than those of Manchester and Glasgow, which require heat and confined air, and clog the lungs with floating particles of cotton. By means of late improvements, the smoke of innumerable coal fires is consumed, and the atmosphere much clearer than formerly. I do not know how far the improvement is applicable to common house fires; if it was, London would gain much by its adoption.

In one place, 500 persons were employed in making plated ware of all sorts, toys and trinkets. We saw there patent carriage steps, flying down and folding up of themselves as the door opens or shuts; chairs in walking-sticks, pocket-umbrellas, extraordinary cheese-toasters, and a multitude of other wonderful inventions, upon which much ingenuity is miserably wasted. In another place, 300 men produce 10,000 gun barrels in a month; we saw a part of the process—enormous hammers, wielded by a steam-engine, of the power of 120 horses, crushing in an instant red hot iron bars, converted into thin ribbons. In that state they are wrapped round a rod of iron, which determines the calibre, and the edges welded together. Bars of iron for different purposes, several inches in thickness, presented to the sharp jaws of gigantic scissars, moved also by the steam-engine, are clipped like paper. Iron wire, from an inch to the tenth of an inch, is spun out with as little effort, and less noise than cotton threads on the jennies. Large millstones, employed to polish metals, turn with so great a velocity as to come to pieces by the mere centrifugal force, and the fragments sometimes pierce the walls or break through the roof; some means have lately been invented to prevent these accidents. Streams of melted metal are poured into moulds of all sorts; and copper is spread into sheets for sheathing vessels under rollers, moved also by the steam-engine, like paste under the stick of the pastry-cook.

Flint glass is a curious manufactory. It is inconceivable with what facility so hard a substance is cut, or rather ground, by the simple friction of a wheel turning with great velocity. The workman presents a decanter, or one of the glass drops of a lustre, to this wheel, and almost as fast as he can move his hand the parts are indented, and form, by the dexterity and justness of his motions, those regular figures we see on the useful or ornamental articles made of that substance. As we stood near the furnace, we observed a stranger approach it, and with an instrument at the end of a long rod of iron, gauge the melted matter in the crucibles. This was, we were told, the exciseman, and his visits are repeated several times a-day. No mark of ill-humour was perceivable. These people are well broken to taxation—they complain indeed, but it is just as they complain of their climate, from habit, or as we see children continue crying, long after they have forgotten the cause of their tears.

This manufactory was lighted by hydrogen gas, and absolutely as light as day. A leaden tube runs round the apartments, with a number of cocks, which, opened more or less, let off a little stream of gas, which is set on fire, and continues burning as long as the cock is open, presenting a bright flame of several inches in length. I counted 120 of these. The gas is obtained from common coals, by mere heat, in a close vessel. This vessel or retort is a cylinder of iron, of about nine inches in diameter, and thirty inches in length; a bushel of coal only is consumed each day. The gas is made to pass through a reservoir of water, which retains the bitumen or coal-tar, and with it the bad smell. Here, however, the smell remained, and was certainly most offensive, but the workmen did not seem to mind it. The reservoir was evidently too small, and the water in it quite saturated; I was told that the gas would lose its inflammability in traversing a greater mass of water, which is I presume an error. The expence of this magnificent illumination is only 4s. 6d. each night, allowing for interest and repairs of the apparatus: 240 candles, affording certainly less light, would cost about twenty times as much—yet this method is not generally adopted, I have not been able to discover why. The manufactory of cut glass has suffered more than most others from the interruption of the trade with the United States; a greater quantity of this showy article being consumed by the *nouveaux riches* of that country than here, where there is certainly much less disposition to extravagance in proportion. Other manufactories suffer more or less by this interruption; for the demand for the United States was undoubtedly very great and increasing. A single house in Birmingham shipped more goods to the United States last year, than was shipped by the whole trade ten years ago; it was indeed after a suspension of eighteen months by the embargo. Merchants now have wholly ceased having goods manufactured for the United States.

Workmen earn from 16 to 60 shillings a week, and even L. 4, according to their skill. They work by the piece—live well and comfortably—have separate houses of three rooms for about L. 5 a year—firing for about one-fifth the price of New York—provisions nearly double. The people look healthy, and the women, of whom many are employed, remarkably well. I observed in neither sex the green hair of which Espriella speaks.* This remark of his seems to have made a greater impression on the good people of Birmingham, than all the other unfriendly things he said of them.

Nothing could exceed the good-nature and politeness with which the chief persons at the principal manufactories showed and

---

* Manuel Alvarez Espriella was the pseudonym chosen by Robert Southey for his *Letters to England* (1808). In volume 1, Letter XXXVI describes the complexion of the people of Birmingham as being "composed of oil and dust smoke-dried. Every man whom I meet stinks of train oil and emery. Some I have seen with red eyes and green hair; the eyes affected by the fires to which they are exposed, and the hair turned green by the brass works. . . ."

explained the processes; and, what is more extraordinary, the workmen stopt in many instances their work (paid by the piece) to give us some practical explanation and answer questions.

March 20.—We went to day to the Leasowes. We were introduced by a hollow way, descending and buried in trees, and soon came to a piece of water of no extent, dull and greenish. Having crossed it by a bridge, we followed the side of it, to a little lake of perhaps six or eight acres, its banks partly woody, partly naked and tame. The house appeared then on our left, at the top of an ascending lawn, with a back-ground of trees, looking like something between a mansion-house and a cottage, and more of the first than we expected; but we found it had been rebuilt since Shenstone's time.* Following a pretty path among trees, we came to a damp and forlorn root-house, in a hollow, where the gardener met us, a poor, old, sickly-looking man, whose uncombed hair was stuck full of feathers. Little able to lead us the round, he gave the key and directions; and then, with a piteous look and low voice, asked *"what we pleased for the poor gardener".* His appearance seemed to suit the neglected state of the place, and his age made me think he might have seen the days of glory of the Leasowes, and assisted in the improvements, and that we might find in him "the sad historian of the pensive plain;" but he had been there only ten years. He told us that the place had been sold or had belonged to thirteen successive owners since Shenstone, most of whom had been ruined; a sad prospect this for improvers and men of taste. I do not see, however, what there should be here so expensive as to ruin any body; it may produce less than a mere farm, and that is all. Before the gardener left us we were treated with water-works. Some unseen lock being opened, the water rushed through a hollow tree, and down a stony declivity, winding about naturally enough, and passing at last under the root-house where we were. The water was extremely dirty, but would be cleaner we were told after a few minutes. It came from the little

---

* William Shenstone (1714–63), the poet, almost ruined himself by the expense of his garden projects at the Leasowes, an estate which he inherited and to which he retired in 1745.

lake we had past. Upon the whole this is rather a pretty place, and nothing more.

We returned to Birmingham, and pursued our journey to Warwick, 20 miles. The road continues improving as we advance south, and instead of stones in coarse fragments, is covered with gravel, always winding about like a stream of water, diverted from its strait course by the slightest obstacle. The English, it is plain, are fond of travelling, and make the pleasure last as long as they can. Gentlemen's grounds, mansions, and genteel cottages, numerous everywhere, seem more so here than ever.

From Warwick we proceeded to Woodstock, 37 miles; a fine fruitful country—avenues of fine elms—large oaks and ash cutting down for timber. I remarked in this part of England, for the first time, the walls of houses and inclosures made of hardened earth; a mode of building very common in the environs of Lyons in France, and called *pisay*. These walls, plastered or rough-cast, last as long as brick. We saw here a company of gypsies, encamped under some ragged canvas stretched on poles. This race, formerly spread all over Europe under the name of Bohemians, is now quite extinct in France, and nearly so in England.

March 22.—Blenheim. This monument of the military glory of Marlborough is close to Woodstock. The entrance to the park is a triumphal-arch, and the *coup-d'oeil*, as soon as you have passed it, is certainly very fine. On the other side of a lake, and sufficiently above it, you see a long range of colonnades, towers, cupolas, and fine trees, with a magnificent stone bridge thrown across a narrow part of the lake, leading to a stupendous column, 150 feet high, bearing a colossal statue of John Churchill, first Duke of Marlborough.

We were first conducted to a small house on the left, containing a humble appendage to the glory of the Marlboroughs, viz. a cabinet or gallery of old china; and were made to undergo the sight of a whole series of dishes and teapots, from the earliest infancy of the art, in modern Europe, among the Romans, and in China: the specimens are, as may be supposed, mostly very coarse, rude, and ugly. Of all *connoisseurships* this is perhaps the most childish. The guardian of these treasures is, very properly, a female. Whether she perceived our unworthiness, I do not know, but there seemed to be a sort of tacit agreement between us to dispatch the business as quickly as possible. Having paid our fees, we drove on, among very fine trees, and, passing between the palace and the water, had a full view of its front, I had heard much of its magnificence, and of its heaviness; but I saw nothing of either.

Crossing the bridge, we admired the finely indented and woody banks of the piece of water, which is very clear, and appears to cover about 200 acres. We drove to the column already mentioned, then across a plain, with meagre plantations, and herds of lazy over-tame deer, round the western extremity of the lake. We had been overtaken by a gardener, who came after us *au grand galop*, mounted on an ass, to direct our admiration to particular spots (all tame enough), and get his 2s. 6d. On the limits of his jurisdiction, the park, he delivered us over to another cicerone, an old servant who descanted on the architecture, and, among other things, made us take notice of a colossal bust of Louis XIV taken at Tournay. He committed us to the charge of another domestic, our fifth guide (a great division of labour), who opened to us a small theatre, used formerly by the family and their friends. A sixth man took us round the pleasure-grounds, and these were certainly well worth seeing.

The seventh guide was a coxcomb of an upper servant, who hurried us through the house. The entrance-hall is very fine. The apartments exhibit Gobelin tapestry, in very bad taste, as usual; a multitude of indifferent pictures, and some good ones. Nothing can be more magnificent than the library. It is about 200 feet long, by 32 feet wide; the coved ceiling is richly worked and painted, and supported by a row of columns of the rarest marbles, each of a single block; the entablature and base also of marble. This library contains 20 or 25,000 volumes. We remarked a statue of Queen Anne by Rysbrack, the dress finished with extreme care. The fees of all our different guides amounted to nineteen shillings. The annual income of the Duke of Marlborough is estimated at L. 70,000. There are eighty house-servants; one hundred out of doors, of whom thirty are for the pleasure-grounds.

From Blenheim to Oxford, eight miles. The first sight of this great university, the antique seat of science, renowned for the splendour of its public edifices, did not answer our expectations. It looked old, dusty, and worm-eaten—the streets silent and deserted—a few students walking lazily, dressed in black gowns and black caps, overshaded with a singular sort of ornament, a thin board, about a foot square, covered with black, and with tassels designating the rank of the scholars. We sent immediately for our ready friend, the little book or guide of the place, which, for two shillings, furnished us a competent allowance of science. Oxford, says the little book, was consecrated to the muses before the Roman conquest. That is certainly going far back; and I should not have supposed that the native Britons knew anything about the muses before Cæsar taught them. At present Oxford does not reckon more than 2000 or 3000 students; and that is a great many.

March 24.—The first approach of Windsor, on a height, is very great and striking. It looks like a castle of Mr Scott's own building, and that is saying enough in its praise. Terraces and towers on high, with banners floating in the wind, sketch their outlines on the sky, while the blast of warlike music comes at intervals on the ear.* Being informed the King was walking, we went that way. His majesty was on the terrace, but the public was not allowed to approach, with a gentleman (General Manners), holding him under the arm. He was dressed in a plain blue coat—his hat flapped over his eyes—stooped a little—looked thin, and walked fast; talking continually, and with an appearance of earnestness. We could at times distinguish his voice at twenty yards distance—this does not look like recovery.†

* Although James Wyatt had supervised some new work on the buildings round the Upper Ward in 1800, the main Gothicisation of Windsor Castle, under the direction of Jeffrey Wyatville, did not take place till the 1820's.

† George III's beloved daughter Amelia had died in the summer of the year before. The old King, evidently suffering from porphyria, appears never to have recovered his reason, except for short intervals, after this final shock.

6

LONDON
25 March 1811 – 25 September 1811

March 25.—London. Here we are once more, after an absence of nine months. This second first sight made much the same impression as the first. London does not strike with admiration; it is regular, clean, convenient, (I am speaking of the best part) but the site is flat; the plan monotonous; the predominant colour of objects dingy and poor. It is altogether without great faults and without great beauties. Suppose yourself in one of the best streets, it extends *à perte de vue* before you, in an undeviating strait line; the side walks wide and smooth; every door with its stone steps, its iron railing, and its lamp; one house differing from its neighbour in no one thing but the number on the door and the name of the occupant. Turn the next corner and you have another street as long, as wide, and as strait, and so on from street to street. At night you have eternal rows of lamps, making the straitness of the streets still more conspicuous and tiresome. This palpable immensity has something in it very heavy and stupifying. The best houses in Edinburgh are very inferior certainly to those of the same rank in London, yet the difference of the materials, a bright crystallized stone, instead of dingy bricks, gives them a look of superior consequence and cheerfulness; the variety of views also, and the proximity to the country, without the fag-end of suburbs, are invaluable advantages. There is no doubt, in London a greater choice of society, the best probably, and the pleasantest; but it is, in general, out of the reach of a stranger, and of no sort of consequence to him.

April 4.—We returned yesterday from Richmond, where we had spent a few days. The spring, which appeared so early, lingers on, and seems at a stand. An easterly wind, dry, acrid, and cold, suspends vegetation. The horse chestnuts are only just out, unfolding their rich gummy bunches of cottony leaves and green pyramids of blossoms in the bud. The hawthorn, larches, and weeping willows just shooting—neither the latter nor the Lombardy poplar grow nearly so fine as in America.

The walk from Richmond to Twickenham by the meadows, along the Thames, is pleasant; but the retrospect of the hill is very inferior indeed to the view from it. After all we have seen in the course of this long tour, this latter view appears to us as beautiful as ever; quite perfect of the kind.

Our friend Mrs D. had the goodness to accompany us to Chiswick, the favourite residence of the Duke of Devonshire, half way between London and Richmond, and consecrated by the death of Mr Fox. This miniature of a palace was built after a design of Palladio, to which, however, wings have been added.* A short avenue of very fine cedars of Lebanon leads to it; one of the trunks, not larger than the rest, measured full twelve feet in circumference—they are only about 80 years old. Three rooms in the centre, lighted by sky-lights, are filled, as almost all the other rooms, with an excellent collection of pictures, as if to make amends for the shocking daubs hanging about the walls of Chatsworth.

April 7.—We went to Westminster Abbey this morning, and found it, with all its merits, inferior to York-Minster, both inside and out. The painted windows are not good; and although I should not wish to white-wash the walls, yet I think them too dark and sooty. The chanting was very fine, and the organ accompaniment simple and beautiful. Whatever sentiments of elevation and piety the music might have produced, were soon unfortunately brought down to the ordinary worldly level by the sermon it was our fortune to hear. The preacher was a purple-faced short-necked man, forcing his hollow, vulgar, insincere voice through a fat narrow passage. He told us, or rather read out of a paper in his hand, that it was wrong to wish to die, yet not right to be afraid neither; and that St Paul taught us to keep a happy medium. Among many words he pronounced in a peculiar manner, I

* Chiswick House (1725–9) was originally built by Lord Burlington. It came into the possession of the 4th Duke of Devonshire, who had married Burlington's heiress, in 1753. The two wings, added by the 5th Duke to the design of James Wyatt in 1788, have now been demolished.

recollect ack*now*ledge and in*no*cence, like *no* in *no*ble, which is not unusual, I think, on the stage; perf*a*dy instead of perfidy; sun-*sine* instead of sun-*shine*.

April 18.—Mr West's new picture at the British Institution is all the fashion at present; everybody goes to see it, and it is considered as his *chef-d'œuvre* after his Regulus. The society has bought the picture for L. 3000. The subject is Christ healing the sick.* They (the sick) form the prominent part of the picture, and certainly they are what they ought to be, very sick. But that is an effect easily produced; and is only an exact likeness of a few wretched objects unconnected and passive.

April 21.—Hamlet was acted yesterday at Covent-Garden, and Kemble, the reigning prince of the English stage, filled the principal part. He understands his art thoroughly, but wants spirit and nature. His manner is precise and artificial; his voice monotonous and wooden; his features are too large, even for the stage. Munden in the part of Polonius, and Fawcett in the grave-digger, played charmingly.† It is enough to mention the grave-diggers, to awaken in France the cry of rude and barbarous taste; and, were I to say how the part is acted, it might be still worse. After beginning their labour, and breaking ground for a grave, a conversation begins between the two grave-diggers. The chief one takes off his coat, folds it carefully, and puts it by in a safe corner; then, taking up his pick-axe, spits in his hand—gives a stroke or two—talks—stops—strips off his waistcoat, still talking—folds it with great deliberation and nicety, and puts it with the coat—then an under-waistcoat, still talking—another and another. I counted

---

* Benjamin West (1738–1820) painted this picture at the age of sixty-five. One of his largest works, it was originally intended for the Quakers in Philadelphia to assist them in building a hospital. Having sold it to the British Institution for £3,000, he sent the Quakers a replica instead.

* Both these comedians had run away from their apprenticeships to go on the stage. Joseph Shepherd Munden (1758–1832) had been apprenticed to a firm of law stationers and had absconded to join a troupe of strolling players. Lamb thought him "not so much a comedian as a company". John Fawcett (1768–1837) had been apprenticed to a linen draper. He specialised in low comedy, and Leigh Hunt knew no one who could "procure so much applause for characters and speeches intrinsically wretched".

seven or eight, each folded and unfolded very leisurely, in a manner always different, and with gestures faithfully copied from nature. The British public enjoys this scene excessively, and the pantomimic variations a good actor knows how to introduce in it, are sure to be vehemently applauded. The French admit of no such relaxation in the *dignité tragique*.

The after-piece was Blue-Beard, which outdoes, in perversion of taste, all the other showy stupidities of the modern stage. A troop of horse (real horse) is actually introduced, or rather two troops, charging each other full speed—the floor is covered with earth—the horses are Astley's, and well drilled; they kick, and rear, and bite, and scramble up walls almost perpendicular, and when they can do no more, fall, and die as gracefully as any of their brethren, the English tragedians. All this might do very well at Astley's, but what a pity and a shame that horses should be the successors of Garrick, and bring fuller houses than Mrs Siddons! *

April 28.—The English have had, for some weeks past, an overflowing of good news from their army in the peninsula. The house of the Portuguese ambassador, has been magnificently illuminated during several nights. These successes are very important in more respects than one—they establish the reputation of the army, heretofore doubtful, and put an invasion of these islands out of the question. The Spanish cause is highly popular in this country—it is a cause to which every generous feeling is associated—and it has excited a great deal of enthusiasm.†

May 1.—Having provided ourselves with a letter of introduction to Mr Lancaster, the celebrated inventor of the new plan of education bearing his name, we drove this morning to his school

---

* Philip Astley (1742–1814) was the most famous horse-trainer in England. In 1770 he started a circus at Lambeth and in 1798 built Astley's Theatre, one of the favourite haunts of the young Dickens. Although Simond is disdainful of the practice, Covent Garden audiences had come to expect that the main production of the evening should be followed by a circus or a pantomime.

† Wellington had spent the winter constructing the lines of Torres Vedras from which Massena, unable to pierce them, had been obliged to withdraw in March with the loss of 30,000 men. On 5 May 1811 Wellington defeated Massena at Fuentes de Oñoro.

in the borough.* We sent in our letter, which was open, and a young monitor coming out, informed us Mr L. was not at home, and we could not be admitted. We represented that we were strangers, and could not possibly come again; and at last, after consulting with other monitors, we were allowed to enter. We found ourselves under a spacious shed, lighted by a sky-light, about 30 or 35 feet wide, and 100 feet long. There was at one end of the extremities a platform, two or three feet above the general level; the rest of the room was paved, and benches arranged one behind the other, fronting the platform, the back of each bench having a shelf serving for a desk for the boy behind; a narrow passage led along the wall, all round the room. Seven or eight hundred boys, from six to twelve years old, filled these benches. They were all talking together and making a great noise. They seemed divided into classes or sections, distinguished by small flags; some of the classes writing on sand, others on slates, that is to say had written, or might have written, for none were doing any thing but playing. Out of compliment to us, for the good of his scholars, or to show his authority, one of the monitors made a sign, and at the instant the eight hundred little heads bowed down, showing instead of a field of white faces, one of dark crops. We asked what the object of this evolution was, and were answered that it was *light and shade*—but what for? Before we could receive a reply, another signal had been given, and all the styles or pencils were brandished in the air—those who had none pointed their finger—at another sign they all came down again. Several other evolutions took place of as little obvious use—a great buz and talking all over the room, and the monitors vociferating. Two boys were lying under a sort of hamper or hen-coop, placed upon the platform; they are there, we were told, for *playing chicken,* that is to say for leaving their places, or playing during the lesson—they did not seem to mind the punishment. Observing some young soldiers with the monitors, we were informed they were sent there to learn the method of the school (not to much purpose this

* Joseph Lancaster (1778-1838) had opened the first of his schools in 1798. It was organised so that the elder boys, the monitors, could take charge of the younger ones and instruct them under Lancaster's supervision.

morning); one of the princes, the Duke of Kent, I believe, having formed the laudable design of a school for the children of soldiers. Thirty or forty new scholars are admitted every week, and they stay two or three years. Such is the information we received from one of the monitors, who did not shew himself a good calculator, for there would be at that rate always a permanent number of 4,500 scholars in the school, which is nearly six times what it can hold. There is a separate school for girls, less numerous, but we did not see it. It struck twelve—the monitor gave the order to clear the school—the boys rose and filed off by benches, making as much noise, and as much dust with their feet as they could.

This is an account of what we saw faithfully reported. I regret it, for it lowers (not much, however,) the very favourable opinion I had formed of the good order, the economy of time, the general application, and prodigious utility of a mode of teaching, by which a single master may direct 1000 scholars, better and more effectually than he could have done ten by any former method. It is obvious that this was not intended as a day to receive visits.

The breweries of London may justly be ranked among its greatest curiosities, and the establishment of Messrs Barclay and Company is one of the most considerable: A steam-engine of the power of 30 horses, does the greatest part of the work; for although there are nearly 200 men employed, and a great number of horses, these are mostly for the outdoor-work; the interior appears quite solitary. Large rakes with chains moved by an invisible power, stir to the very bottom the immense mass of malt in boilers 12 feet deep; elevators which nobody touches, carry up to the summit of the building 2500 bushels of malt a day, thence distributed through wooden channels to the different places where the process is carried on. Casks of truly gigantic sizes are ready to receive the liquors. One of them contains 3000 barrels. Now, at eight barrels to a ton, this is equal to a ship of 375 tons. By the side of this are other enormous vessels, the smallest of which, containing about 800 barrels, are worth, when full, L. 3000 Sterling each. This fleet of ships is hung up upon a frame of timbers so as to walk freely under them, and render all parts accessible, the whole under a common roof. The stock of liquor is estimated at L. 300,000; the barrels alone in which it is carried about to the consumers cost L. 80,000; and the whole capital is not less than half a million sterling: 250,000 barrels of beer are sold annually, which would load a fleet of 150 merchantmen of the burden of 200 tons each. The building is incombustible; walls of brick and floors of iron. Messrs Barclay and Company are the successors of Thrale, whose name is associated to the immortality of Johnson; and the words of the philosopher occurred naturally to us at sight of the very objects by which they had been suggested.* More than 100 horses are employed in carrying the beer to the consumers. We saw a number of them in a long range of stables. These colossusses are fed with a mixture of clover, hay, straw, and oats, chopped together very fine, so as to enable horses ever so old to feed without difficulty. They are often sixteen hours in harness out of the twenty-four. There was not one sick. They looked prodigiously square and heavy; more so, I should think, than is best for use. We took notice that the steam-engine did not make the least noise—not more than a clock; you might have heard a pin drop all over the building.

May 7.—Those persons who have a box at the opera by the year, may fill it with whom they please; and they actually retail out their seats when they do not go themselves. There is a bookseller's shop in Bond Street, where tickets of private boxes are always to be had, sometimes below, and sometimes above the standing price, as it happens to be a good or a bad day. Saturday, for instance, is a fashionable day, and you are asked sometimes two guineas for a ticket, while, on a vulgar day, it is eight shillings only, (the established price is 10s. 6d.). On benefit nights every

* It is one of the most charming of all Boswell's stories. Johnson, to his great pride, had been appointed an executor of Thrale's vast estate, and Boswell "could not but be somewhat diverted by hearing Johnson talk in a pompous manner of his new office, and particularly of the concerns of the brewery, which it was at last resolved should be sold . . . when the sale was going forward, Johnson appeared bustling about, with an ink-horn and pen in his button-hole, like an excise-man; and on being asked what he really considered to be the value of the property which was to be disposed of, answered, 'we are not here to sell a parcel of boilers and vats, but the potentiality of growing rich beyond the dreams of avarice.' "

body pays; fashionable people do not go then, and their boxes are filled with plebeians. There is another sort of shabby saving sanctioned by fashion. It is not uncommon for fine people going out of town to let their houses furnished for the time of their absence. This profanation of the household gods furnishes a few guineas more to spend in vain ostentation the following season. Nobody thinks of writing to a friend without a frank, and letters are received with a perceivable expression of surprise, at least, when there is postage to pay. You may pay the postage of your own letters; and I had availed myself of the expedient, as infinitely preferable to that of begging a frank, but I found it was considered as a great impropriety.

May 9.—Astley's is an equestrian *spectacle*. I supposed that a thing of that sort would be particularly good in England, which is a sort of island of the Houyhnhnms. I found, however, that the horses were but indifferently trained, and the men performed only common feats; and, instead of equitation, we had dramatic pieces and Harlequin tricks—battles and assaults—Moors and Saracens. The horses performed as actors, just as at Covent Garden; they galloped over the pit, and mounted the boards of the stage covered with earth, storming walls and ramparts. The interval between the exhibitions being very long, a parcel of dirty boys (amateurs), in rags, performed awkward tricks of tumbling, raising a cloud of dust, and showing their nakedness to the applauding audience; the vociferations from the gallery were perfectly deafening, and the hoarse vulgar voice of the clown eagerly re-echoed by them. Looking round the room, meanwhile, I saw the boxes filled with decent people—grave and demure citizens, with their wives and children, who seemed to take pleasure in all this. It is really impossible not to form an unfavourable opinion of the taste of the English public, when we find them in general so excessively low and vulgar in the choice of their amusements.

May 11.—Wishing to see the lions of Westminster Abbey, we went there this morning. It was near the end of the service; there was only *one* person in the church—a woman. After the service, a sexton collected the curious, who had come on the same errand as ourselves, and led us the accustomed round, enumerating the various monuments in his way, ancient and modern, in marble, in wood, in brass—most of them very bad indeed. The one of Sir Isaac Newton, by Rysbrack, is fine.

There is an odd collection of antique personages of illustrious fame or royal rank, of their natural size, in wood and wax, and covered with tawdry and tattered garments, as shabby as possible; the whole quite barbarous. At last, however, the door of one of the presses being opened, shewed us Lord Nelson, his size and make and habitual attitude well imitated, dressed in the clothes he had worn, to the very shoes and buckles on them, and a perfect likeness. We had just been reading his life by Clarke and Macarthur, and this figure of the hero was so like life—so much more so than sculpture or painting could make it, that it struck us deeply. There was in that little body, so worn out and mutilated—in the shrunk, furrowed countenance and melancholy aspect—something wonderfully impressive.

Sir Francis Burdett had made us miss the Tower last year, and, proverbially vulgar as it is to see the Tower and its lions, we set off to go there early this morning, being a journey of full six miles, through the whole length of the town. The Tower is an irregular assemblage of buildings of various sorts, surrounded by a wall and large moat full of water, in a circumference of about 1200 feet, forming an area of three or four acres. The principal tower, which gives its name to all the rest, was built by William the Conqueror, as a place of safety in case of insurrection. Its site being rather elevated, it overlooks the town and river. Since that time state criminals have been put there. When condemned to death they were executed on Tower-Hill, and buried in the chapel, but without their heads, which were reserved to sweeten the air of Temple Bar.

The jewels of the crown or regalia are kept in a strong room by themselves—we escaped them, and our last station was the menagerie, which is small, ill-contrived, and dirty. The animals look sick and melancholy. The most curious of them was a white tiger, lately brought from India by Sir Edward Pellew, and so tame, that the sailors used to pare his claws regularly during the voyage, and on his landing, he was led through some of the streets of London, or rather followed like a dog.

Returning from the Tower, we stopped at Guildhall. The entrance-hall is disfigured by the two huge barbarous figures, called Gog and Magog, and not much ornamented by a recent monument to the memory of Lord Nelson. How many monuments to this hero we have met in England, and not one in America to the memory of Washington!

May 16.—Mr Brand's motion for Parliamentary reform was to come before the House of Commons yesterday—[we] went there very early (12 o'clock). We took our stand on the stairs, expecting a crowd. A postponement of the question being, however, soon after whispered about, many of the expectants went away, and at near four we got in without much difficulty. I had an order of admission from a Member of Parliament, but it was easy to perceive that a bank-token (a silver piece worth 5s. 6d.) was more welcome to the door-keeper. This payment is done openly, and you may change a bank-note at the door of the gallery of the House of Commons as you would at the door of the playhouse. There is in this an appearance of indelicacy certainly, but the object is to throw some difficulty in the way of mere idle curiosity, and check the concourse of the lower class. This payment of money answers the purpose nearly as well as the necessity of obtaining an order from a member. Mr Brand did, as was expected, postpone his motion till next month. After some previous business, a short debate took place respecting public schools in Ireland. A dapper little man, with a very sharp nose and chin, spoke most, and in a confused manner, from behind the treasury-bench—he stated some curious facts about a shameful evasion on the part of the English clergy in Ireland, who, although bound to have schools in each parish, got off by paying 40s. a-year to some person, unable often to read himself, who pretended to keep a school. This disclosure seemed candid on the part of a supporter of the English hierarchy. Another little man, as thin as a shadow, and drawing one side of his body after him, as if paralytic, hurried across the floor with a tottering brisk step, and awkward bow, and said in substance, that schools in Ireland were most desirable, and should be organized by all means. These few words were extremely well spoken, with peculiar energy of feeling, and in a manner graceful and impressive. This was Mr Wilberforce. Nothing can surpass the meanness of his appearance, and he seems half blind. Next, another shadow (and well they may be shadows, who work all day in the cabinet, and wrangle all night, baited like bears at the stake) the chancellor of the Exchequer, very small features, and sallow complexion, his voice low, but distinct, and flowing smoothly on without hesitation, and without warmth—the subject indeed required none (something about duties on foreign spirits).*

Parliamentary oratory is a thing totally different from the style of public speaking in France, not at all haranguing or reciting, but rather like an argumentative and uninterrupted conversation. Eloquent appeals to the imagination or the passions, seem to arise spontaneously from the subject, without being sought for—a momentary burst, rather checked than encouraged. The speaker returns, as soon as possible, to a simple unimpassioned style, and to the business before the House, or rather never loses sight of it. Plain facts are the elements of his eloquence. He brings them together, places them in a strong light, and lets them speak for themselves. He aims at a vigorous and correct sketch—not a laboured picture. Mr [Samuel] Whitbread made a sortie against the Scotch member. I was glad of an opportunity of hearing one of the most formidable champions of liberty in the British senate. He spoke of course against the excessive issue of paper-money, and in favour of specie payments, which are the dogma of the party. I found Mr Whitbread much as I expected, a stout man, brisk, rather rough, with more force than taste. His irony borders on invective.

The house was very thin. I counted several times only 20, never more than 70 members—the quorum is forty; but the deficiency is not noticed by the chair, unless a member points it out. The two clerks of the House, in black gowns and powdered wigs, sat at the table before the speaker. Full half the time of one of them was taken up in placing the mace upon the table when the speaker of the House took the chair, and under the table when he left it; the chairman of the committee then taking his seat at the table by the

* The Chancellor of the Exchequer at this time was Spencer Percival (1762–1812). From 1809 until his murder in 1812 he was also Prime Minister.

clerks. When he does this, first leaving his seat at the treasury-bench, he goes half way down to the door of the house, then, turning back, makes a bow to the chair, and, retracing his steps, reaches his *chairman's seat* at the table, close to his other seat, as member, which he had just left. Seen from the gallery, this looks much like a boy practising before the dancing-master. Members moving or going away, but not on coming in, make bows also, generally very awkward ones. A message was brought from the upper house by two personages in gowns and wigs. One of the clerks took the mace and went to receive them at the door, and brought them to the table, bowing; when, after delivering some papers, they retreated backwards the whole way, and bowing, clerk, mace, and all. It was a great relief to me to see them reach the door in safety, for I half-expected they would, by treading back upon their trains, tumble down upon the floor; but they went through their exercise like practised *figuranti* at the opera.

About half after two in the morning, the gallery was cleared—that is to say, the public ordered out, which we could not be very sorry for, after eleven hours of the same constrained attitude. We adjourned to the kitchen, a very clean and spacious one, much frequented by the honourable members. Small tables stood along the wall; a cloth was laid for us on one of them. Three successive beef-steaks were broiled under our eyes, over a clear strong fire, incessantly turned, and served good and hot, tender, delicate, and juicy. This is a national dish, rarely good; but under this national roof it proved excellent. Duly restored by this and a bottle of port wine, we were about returning to the House, when we found it had adjourned.

May 17.—The Hay-Market Theatre is precisely of the proper dimensions to hear and see. Elliston, who is an excellent actor, filled the principal part in an indifferent play, the subject of which is taken from the story of Cardenio in Don Quixote.* There is, however, a very affecting scene in it, that in which the unfortunate madman meets the mistress he had lost, without knowing her. Some faint recollections seem excited by her presence, and awaken

* Robert William Elliston (1774–1831). Leigh Hunt judged him the "best lover on the stage".

his attention—he contemplates her long in uneasy silence—remembrance, at last, and reason beam upon his disordered mind—he rushes towards his mistress and falls senseless at her feet. The shades of returning intelligence and sentiment—the passage from stupid indifference to passionate feelings, have been represented with great skill. The hysterical laugh is a legitimate means of expressing what could not be expressed half so well otherwise; but that heart-rending sound must be introduced very sparingly, and may easily become ridiculous instead of affecting. Elliston repeated it three different times: it was once, at least, too often.

Among the curiosities of London, the cabinet of Natural History, known under the name of the Liverpool Museum, deserves to be mentioned. The boa constrictor is a gigantic snake, which makes the story of Laocoon quite probable. This one crushes a deer in its ample folds, and tears it to pieces with its teeth; it is about 35 feet in length, and as large as a man's thigh. The giraffe is another prodigious animal. A quadruped 16 feet high, with a very pretty head like a horse, and mild innocent look, at the top of an immensely long, yet graceful, crane neck. This animal is singularly gifted to discover all approaching danger from his tower of observation, and to fly from it with his seven league boots. A moderate-sized elephant near him, looked quite small.

There are new panoramas this year at Mr Parker's, as admirable as those he exhibited the last. We have just seen Malta. The gairish light of day, white and dazzling—the strong and perpendicular shadows—the dusty land—the calm and glassy sea, paint heat to the eye. The inhabitants overcome, lie about in the shade of narrow streets—a sentinel alone is seen pacing his watch before the gate of the arsenal. The smallest details are characteristic, and represented with perfect truth, and, at the same time, with poetical taste and feeling. We learned, with much regret, that the panorama of Dover, which we admired so much last year, was painted on this identical cloth. Malta is laid over Dover, and Dover covers half-a-dozen more *chefs-d'œuvre*! I should be much tempted to rescue a few of them if I could, and carry off some of Mr Parker's canvas as Lord Elgin has done Phidias's marbles.

The circumference of the panorama is about 270 feet, the height 30 feet, the surface about 900 square yards.

May 22.—The expected meeting between [Tom] Molineaux, the black, from America, and a Lancashire pugilist (Rimmer) took place yesterday. These sorts of combats being peculiar to the country, I wished to be present at one of them, and repaired early to the field, (Molesey Hurst, near Hampton Court, 15 miles from London,) with Mr S. who had the goodness to accompany me. We found an immense ring already formed—a sort of Scythian entrenchment of carts and waggons, arranged side by side in double and treble rows, without horses. This is a contrivance of the country people, who speculate on the curiosity of the Londoners, and let their elevated vehicles to the amateurs of the fist. We made our bargain, and mounted a cart, whence we had a full view of the immense crowd already assembled inside the ring of carts, in the centre of which we could see a smaller ring, perhaps 40 feet across, surrounded with stakes and a rope. About half after twelve o'clock, Rimmer appeared in the ring, a tall, good-looking young man, with a high colour. The black arrived soon after, mounted on the box of a barouche and four, with some young men of fashion; he was muffled up in great-coats, and seemed a clumsy-looking fellow. Here began a scene quite unexpected to me, the clearing of the ring. All the boxers in town, professional and amateurs, charged the mob at once, which giving way in confusion, formed a sort of irregular circle outside the rope-ring, but not large enough. With sticks and whips applied, *sans cérémonie*, these champions of the fist pressed back the compact mass. I expected every moment a general engagement—nothing of the kind; the mob shrunk from the flogging, but without resentment. Tis true the blows appeared to be directed mostly over the heads of the first ranks, and fell on those five or six deep; the weapons being mostly coachmens or carters long whips. These rear ranks, assailed by an invisible hand, had no resource but a retreat, and made way for those in front; the latter, squatting down on the turf, formed, at last, a sort of barrier over which the crowd could see. The combatants soon stripped; the black exhibiting the arms, breast, and shoulders of Hercules, with the "head, scarce more extensive than the sinewy neck;" his legs also extremely muscular, and not much of the negro make. The Lancashire man, taller, and broader, but not so deep, square, and muscular, appeared undaunted, and had lost none of his colour. They shook hands and stood on their defence, shy to begin for some minutes. I could not tell who gave the first blow, so quickly was it returned. The Lancashire man fell and fell again. One of the rounds he closed with the black, threw him, and fell over himself. Twice more, I think, he attempted to wrestle, with various success, but was often knocked down. His left eye appeared closed, and he was all stained with blood—I could not well distinguish where it came from. The blood was not so visible on the skin of the black, but I observed that he was much more out of breath than his adversary. At every round, which is generally terminated by a fall, the seconds raise their friend—wipe the blood—bathing his temples with a sponge dipped in vinegar and water. The champion who did not fall sits in the meantime on the bended knee of one of his seconds, leaning upon him, to take as much rest as he can, and is refreshed also by sponging. The battle had lasted half an hour—about twenty rounds—the Lancashire-man always thrown; when all at once the barrier was broken—an irruption of the mob took place, and soon became general, rushing towards the centre, and overwhelming the ring and its occupants. I lost sight of the combatants. Whips and sticks were lifted up in vain—there was not even room to strike. All was clamour, and struggle, and confusion, for twenty minutes. At last we saw the ropes and stakes taken away, as if any further battle was out of the question, or an adjournment intended to some other spot. Unwilling to lose their sport, the mob seemed to give way a little, and had no sooner made an opening, than a desperate charge drove them back to their former situation, where squatting again, order was restored, and the combatants stood. The white man seemed still able and stout, but fell like an ox under the club of the butcher at the first round —at the second—and so on, from bad to worse, rising each time with more difficulty. It became a shocking sight. Victory was out of the question, and had been so almost from the beginning. His better wind might have afforded him a chance—he had lost it by the interruption. The black was now fresh—he pressed his exhausted adversary, retreating before him. At last a knock-down blow laid him prostrate near the ring of spectators (for the rope-ring was gone). In vain his seconds, exerting themselves about him, raised him from the ground; his head hung on his breast—he could not stand—he appeared *hors de combat*—and the prescribed time to face his adversary having expired (two or three minutes), victory was declared on the other side. Hats flew—cries rent the air; the black, meantime, grinning over his fallen adversary in savage triumph! The mob rushed in from all parts; and we rushed out; not wishing to see any more—and, finding our vehicle, drove back to London.

This was not deemed a good battle. Young Rimmer overrated his own strength, and has received a good lesson for his temerity. The black will not meet with many pugilists equal to him in point of muscle, but he wants wind and coolness; he puts himself in a passion, and will be beat by the professors, if he dares try them. A pleasing reflection softened the brutality of this sight; it was the impartiality with which the populace observed the *loi du combat*, and saw one of their own people thus mauled and bruised by a foreigner and a negro, suffering him to enjoy his triumph unmolested; for the interruption had been a mere ebullition of curiosity and enthusiastic admiration for the art—not ill-will or unfair interference. When I call this collection of people populace, I do not mean that they were all low people; there were no ragged coats in sight, and half the mob were gentlemen.

We have spent a few days with some of our friends in Hertfordshire, 20 miles north of London. For half that distance you travel between two rows of brick houses, to which new ones are added every day; their walls are frightfully thin, a single brick of eight inches—and, instead of beams, mere planks lying on an edge. I am informed, it is made an express condition in the leases of these shades of houses, that there shall be no dances given in them; and, as if to destroy the little solidity of which such thin walls are susceptible, they generally place a window above the pier below, and a pier above the window below. London extends its great polypus-arms over the country around. The population is not increased by any means in production to these appearances—only transferred from the centre to the extremities. This centre is become a mere counting-house, or place of business. People live in the outskirts of the town in better air—larger houses—and at a smaller rent—and stages passing every half hour, facilitate communications. Certain parts of these extremities of the town are, however, exposed to a great nuisance; the air is poisoned by the emanation from brick-kilns, exactly like carrion, to such a degree, as to excite nausea, and the utmost disgust, till the cause of the smell is known; when the immediate relief experienced, shews how much imagination and association have to do with what seems mere sensation. As soon as we got beyond the sight and the smell of bricks the country appeared to great advantage. Green fields and hedge-rows all around us; and on the right, at some distance, a range of very pretty hills, well wooded, and with gentlemen's houses here and there on the slope. These hills are, I believe, part of the site of Epping Forest, as it is called; of which, as of most other English forests (the New Forest excepted), not a vestige seems to remain.

The East India Company formed here a few years ago a magnificent establishment, for the education of young men destined to its service.* The college is a quadrangle, about 400 feet every way, inclosing an area of four acres of grass, around which the apartments of the students and halls for the lectures are distributed. The principal front presents a long low line, adorned with three pediments; the one in the middle, supported by six columns, is tacked to a dead wall, and leads to nothing; the two end ones are, on the contrary, all open, and the light is seen through. Neither the one nor the other look very well. This edifice is built of Portland-stone, on a rising ground, with a gravelled terrace before it—a sloping lawn—and a background of trees.

There are at present ninety young men in the college, from 15 to 18 years of age, and the number increasing, who all have an appointment in the Company's service. They pay L. 100 a-year—board and lodging in the house, and even washing, are included.

* This school, now Haileybury College, was founded in 1805 by the East India Company and at that time housed in Hertford Castle.

They have each a small room with a fire-place, and a recess for a bed—no fees to the professors, whose lectures they attend three hours a-day. The rest of their time is taken up with reading and preparing themselves for the lectures, or rather for the examinations, which seem to be very strict and effectual. They have to answer questions on their different studies in writing, without leaving the room, without consulting any books, and without knowing beforehand the precise questions, although they know the subjects in general upon which they are to be examined. I saw in the hands of one of the professors (the author of the celebrated Essay on Population,) a number of these manuscripts, passing every day under his eyes, containing often twenty or thirty pages, on political economy and history, some of them extremely good. The corrections and comments of the professor are also in writing; and although he does not, upon the whole, lecture more than five hours in a week, his time is fully employed. There are eight professors, besides the principal. The professor of Sanscrit, Mr Hamilton, is first-cousin of our General Hamilton, the most distinguished character in the United States after Washington.

The examination of witnesses, now going on before a committee of the House of Commons, respecting the causes of the distresses of manufacturers, and the means of relief, has produced the disclosure of some curious facts.* For instance, the wages of weavers at Glasgow are now reduced to one-fourth of what they were nineteen years ago, although the price of provisions and other necessaries has doubled in the mean time! This is not wholly occasioned by the late interruptions of trade, but has been gradually coming on. The system of throwing a number of small farms into a few large ones—the various improvements in agriculture, saving labour—and above all sheep-farming, had, for many years past, tended to reduce the demand for men in the country; while the rapid increase of manufacturers created a demand in the towns, and a consequent rise of wages. At last the extended application of machinery, par-

* The Committee had been set up after the Commons had received a petition containing 40,000 signatures from the cotton manufacturers in the north. The Committee's report was inconclusive and ineffectual.

ticularly the steam-engine, to manufactures, and the continual influx of population from the country to the towns, reduced successively the great difference there was nineteen years ago, between the respective salaries of town and country, and the late crisis of commerce has added to the existing causes of distress, but has not been the only one. Labourers, placed between the steam-engine in town, and sheep in the country, are threatened with starvation amid systems of real plenty. The remedies proposed by the deputations of workmen are all absurd, such as a *minimum* of prices for their labour—taxes on machines, &c. &c. The fact is, there are too many labourers; and the only remedy is, for a less number of young men to take to the loom, and a greater number to shoulder the musket, and to go on board ship. These commercial difficulties have an evident tendency to increase the effectual force of England.

The Marquis of Salisbury has a fine house, or rather palace, about ten miles west of Hertford (Hatfield house). Its first appearance is quite baronial, and very striking. Elizabeth resided there some time before she came to the throne, and the architecture is in the taste of that age. A great brick quadrangle, with windows innumerable, round, square, or in a bow, and of all colours; the top *herissé* with turrets and belfrys; but, upon the whole, and although there is a want of breadth of surface and simplicity, it is a magnificent edifice. As we reached the door, and looked back, the vast lawn descending every way, and the prodigiously fine trees—the remains of an avenue—and dispersed everywhere, had as great and pleasing an effect as any thing of the sort we have yet seen in England. There was some doubt whether we should be admitted, as the Duke of Clarence was expected next day on a visit, the Marquis of S. being already come to receive his noble visitor, and the whole house in the full tide of preparation. But the servants, good souls, are very unwilling to disappoint strangers, and we saw all.

June 2.—We had the pleasure of being present to-day when the widow of a hero (Sir Ralph A.) received the news of the safety of her son, after the dreadful battle of Badajos, where every fourth man, and more than that proportion of officers, were killed or wounded. This happy mother heard, at the same time, of her son having greatly distinguished himself, in this his first action.* The English are in a fair way of showing to the rest of Europe that they are not that *nation boutiquière* they were taken for. Their enemies have *dechalandé* the shop, and its *courtands* have turned soldiers. I have often thought that if France had been allowed, at a certain period, to take to the shop again, that is to say, to resume the arts and occupations of peace, it might have proved the best security for the rest of Europe.

June 10.—Grand review on Wimbledon Common. The Prince Regent was to be on the ground at eleven o'clock. We arrived a little after nine, and wedged in our carriage among innumerable others, which, with carts and waggons, formed a circle of full six or eight miles in circumference. The troops were drawn up in two parallel lines across it, of about two miles in length. The Prince did not appear till near twelve. He was on horseback, looked fat and fair, but was too far off to be seen distinctly. The sun being extremely hot and some heavy clouds portending rain, the people were impatient, and murmured at the delay. The effect of the running fire beginning at one end of the line ending two miles off, and returning, and then again repeated, had a fine effect; the review was not otherwise worth seeing, the distance being too great, and no manœuvring. The troops were about 20,000, and the spectators full 200,000. Some light-horsemen rode continually around the circle, and repressed the intruding multitude with some degree of unavoidable rudeness, though much less than the keepers of the ring at the boxing-match the other day, nor would the people have borne so patiently similar discipline.

The general orders for the review, printed and published, enjoined the troops to *avoid as much as possible giving any offence to individuals*. There were a few accidents from horses taking fright at the firing.

June....—Albury. We have been here for some days, in a very pretty country, already described last year, and where the kind attention of other friends, and the virtue of strawberries, are likely

---

* Sir Ralph Abercombie was mortally wounded in 1801 after the landing at Aboukir Bay. The son to whom Simond refers was his youngest, Alexander (1784–1852).

to complete my recovery. Before a stranger ventures to pass final sentence on the anti-social manners of the English, he should see them at home in the country. London is not their home; it is an encampment for business and pleasure, where every body thinks of himself. You might as well look for humanity in a field of battle, as for urbanity and attentions in a busy crowd.

This is sheep-shearing time, which in England is a sort of festivity, like the *moisson* in the north of France, and the *vendange* in the south, and the principal harvests in all countries. The sack of wool, on which the Chancellor sits in Parliament, is well known to be emblematic of the importance of this production. The mirth and festivity of the people here is quite calm, and a *fête* after their manner might, in Languedoc, be mistaken for a funeral. If the country people dance, it is without elasticity, vivacity, or ardour; if they sing, it is far worse. Nothing ever was less musical than the indigenous English music, with its jerks and starts, jolting along its rugged way, without either dignity, liveliness, or tenderness—so different from the native Scotch music, which possesses at least one of these modes of expression, and from the Italian music, which unites them all. Italian music is now naturalized in England; but it will not supersede the old tavern music so entirely as it did in France the flat old style; and, so far as it is connected with naval enthusiasm, it is perhaps better it should be so. The native music of the southern extremity of France formed an exception to the dulness of the national musical taste, as that of North compared to South Britain.

A good sheep-shearer dispatches four or five sheep in an hour, or forty in a day; three pounds is an average fleece—five or six pounds a very large one. The sheep is not tied during the operation, and does not struggle much. The body is placed in such a situation as to stretch the skin of the parts under the shears, which might otherwise inflict wounds. The animal is kept covered for a few nights afterwards. The people abused Merino sheep, and said they would not do with them. There is probably a great deal of prejudice in this opinion, which must, however, have gained ground, as the price of that breed has fallen as much too low as it had perhaps risen too high before.

I have seen here larches, planted only sixty years ago, the trunks of which were nine feet in circumference, and 80 feet in height, the sweeping boughs extending full 30 feet every way. An oak, 25 or 30 years old, is worth L. 3, at the rate of four or five shillings a cubic foot, and in 15 years doubles its value. I have seen an oak for which the sum of L. 140 has been refused.

The soil is chalk, and not very fertile, renting on an average at 20s. an acre; good meadows rent at three times that price. Estates sell at thirty years purchase. Labourers earn 2s. 3d. and 2s. 6d. in summer, 2s. in winter. Poor's rates 4s. in the pound! The peasants look very decent in their manners, dress, and appearance. No marks of poverty about them; but they are certainly very diminutive in stature, and thin. They seem better clothed and fed. One might suspect that a certain native pride in them disdains to wear the livery of poverty, although they suffer in secret. The quartern loaf of bread (4 lb. 5 oz.) costs 1s. 0½d.; it was, in 1794 and 1795, 1s. 10½d.; that is, nearly double the present high price! The highest price of bread in scarce years in France has been, I believe, six sous a-pound, equal to about half the highest price above mentioned, yet the people suffered more there; they were, and they are poorer than here.

The Prince Regent has given a very magnificent fête, which was the object of general conversation for a fortnight.* It was computed that 1600 persons invited, supposed, at least, 400 carriages; and that allowing two minutes for each, more than 13 hours would be required for the whole number to be delivered at the door; and that beginning at eleven o'clock at night, it would take till twelve the next day! His Majesty having heard of the intended fête, is said to have asked whether he might not be permitted to go as a private gentleman. This raillery is in the same spirit with another *bon-mot* of this august patient. "*Here you see me,*" he said, to a

---

* This fête, which was said to have cost £120,000, was given on 19 June. For three days afterwards, the public were admitted to inspect the rooms where it had been held. On the last day, 30,000 people endeavoured to get in. There was a stampede and ladies, according to one account, "were to be seen all round the gardens, most of them without shoes or gowns; and many almost completely undressed, and their hair hanging about their shoulders".

person who approached him, in a moment of personal restraint, indispensable in his situation, *"check-mated."*

June 21.—The fête went off very well. The difficulties had been obviated by opening several avenues—the Prince was most gracious —he spoke to all, and delighted everybody by the courtesy of his manners, although courtesy is out of fashion.

A sort of decoration, on the good taste of which I shall not pronounce, led to a tragi-comic occurrence. There was a stream of water, real water, which had been made to flow, I do not know by what means, along the middle of the table, in a meandering channel, with proper accompaniments of sand, moss, and rocks, in miniature, and bridges across. Gold and silver fishes frisking about in the stream, exhibited the brightness of their scales, reflecting the light of 500 flambeaux, to the infinite delight of the guests. When at the height of their honours and glory, the greatest any of their kind ever attained before, they were seen, with astonishment and dismay, to turn on their backs, the one after the other, and to expire, without anybody being able to guess at the cause.

The apartments where the fête was given, were open to the public the next day. Curiosity was extreme, quite as much so as it might have been at Paris. The people, and not the low people, went in crowds to Carleton-House. This affluence had not been foreseen, nor any precautions taken; and there have been many very serious accidents. People have been thrown down and trodden under foot—arms and legs have been fractured—ribs forced in— and, it is said, some lives lost. Many a delicate female was extricated from the *mêleé*, nearly *in naturalibus*, and obliged to hide herself in a corner till petticoats could be procured; as to shoes no lady pretended to keep them; and after the event, they were swept in heaps, and filled, we have been told, several hogsheads.

June 26.—Winchester. We took leave of our friends this morning, and are come here to sleep, (42 miles). I am astonished at the prodigious extent of waste grounds in a country depending for food on the granaries of its enemies, and having 50 or 60 thousand idle prisoners of war to support, who, I dare say, would be very glad to work for a small salary, besides innumerable paupers, supported by means of an enormous tax on the public. We traversed to-day several extensive downs, used only as sheep pastures. The chalk stratum is covered with a few inches of vegetable mould, and would be well worth cultivating. When the general inclosure bill was before parliament in 1793, the quantity of waste land was estimated at 22 millions of acres, about two-fifths of the surface of the whole island. Supposing one-half to have been inclosed and cultivated since that time, there would still be one-fifth waste. If the present population was perfectly at their ease on the other four-fifths, I certainly would not wish to see these fine green downs furrowed by the plough, and vulgar lines of property disfigure their surface; but if the generation wants bread, it seems very absurd not to let them grow it here. I know the next generation will not be better off, and that twenty years hence they would again want space; but for the men of the present day, the palliative is a complete cure.

Near Winchester, we passed several depôts of French prisoners—the officers on their parole, wandering *désœuvrés* and tired about the streets and roads. Winchester is of course old, and ugly—the cathedral is fine.

June 27.—Southampton. The country near this place begins to look *forestish*. Cottages, as usual, neat, and overgrown with roses and honeysuckle, though ever so poor; a bit of lawn and gravel-walk to the door, an imitation of gentlemen's cottages. Southampton has only one street of any consequence, and a walk planted with stunted trees along the bay. Nothing can surpass the dirt and bad smells of the bye streets; the tide leaving putrescent quagmires all about the lower parts. A very singular edifice proudly overlooks this dirty town. It is a castle, large, Gothic, prodigiously high, surrounded by lofty walls of hewn stones. It cost L. 40,000, and is not finished. Not an inch of ground beyond these walls. The meanest hovels crowd around them, and the view extends over a field of red-tile roofs and chimneys, to the slimy banks of Southampton bay; the New Forest, forming a long, low unpicturesque strait line beyond it. Lord Lansdown, lately dead, built this castle. He was a very tall and thin man, riding on a long lean horse, and had following him a very little page, called his dwarf, mounted on a diminutive poney. The knight, the dwarf, and the castle, seemed made for each other. He must, in the main, have been a good sort of man, as the people about here, although they laugh at the castle and castle-builder, all speak well of him, and are hardly willing to admit that he was mad; but then, as I have observed before, the qualifications required for acknowledged insanity, are by no means easily attained in England, where a greater latitude is granted for whims, fancies, and eccentricities, than in other countries.*

June 2.—Isle of Wight. Cowes is a pretty place, with many gentlemen's houses near it as usual. One of them is a gothic castle —bran-new—stuck round with towers and battlements. Not far from it a poorer neighbour has erected his own Gothic thatched cottage.

The Gothic style is considered here as national, and certainly they use it freely, and as their own. Horace Walpole contributed, I fancy, to spread the taste and the misapplication of it.

Traversing the island through the middle of it, we are returned to our beautiful Under-cliff, with an intention of spending a few days there. The middle of the island by Newport, its capital, is, like all the rest, woody, fertile, and flourishing.

July 6. Steephill.—We have taken lodgings for a week in a fisherman's cottage—a sort of an ale-house. It has been a perfect calm at sea for some days, which is unfavourable for fishing. Five or six boats have, in consequence, come to an anchor near here, and the men, who are idle, have spent their time in a room adjoining ours, drinking, or near the house playing at bowls. They sung frequently, two or three voices together, sea-songs in the true sailor style— sometimes extremely well, oftener very badly—altogether it was not to be borne long, and we were going away, when the wind arose, and they disappeared. This gave us, however, an opportunity of observing a new class of people, and, much to their credit, we found them remarkably well-behaved, and decent, although noisy —no quarrels among themselves, and no absolute drunkenness. I

---

* William Petty, 2nd Earl of Shelburne and 1st Marquess of Lansdown (then spelled without an e) (1737–1805) began work on Southampton Castle in the year of his death. His son, John Henry Petty Fitzmaurice (1765–1809) continued the work and employed John Linnell Bond to design him a room in the Moorish style.

was surprised to find their fishing-tackle were made of osier, but not exactly the sort with which baskets are made—the withy rope, as they call it, lasts good two years, although continually wet and dry; a hempen rope would hardly last so long, would cost ten times the price, and be much heavier. It makes also very good cables for light boats, and fastened to posts, makes inclosures. Taking advantage of the opportunity, I learnt the art of withy rope making, and shall carry a sample of this economical manufacture to America.

Wheat grows extremely well on this perturbed soil, mostly chalk—it is in many places a man's height. Potatoes and all other crops seem to succeed equally well. The low pastures are covered with fine Alderney cows, and the steep downs with sheep. Our guide-book informs us that this fortunate island yields seven times as much as its inhabitants consume. It enumerates all the cheeses, and all the sheep and cattle exported to London market; and tells of a butcher who bought 1500 lambs at one purchase. However that may be, our fare here is very much confined to crabs, lobsters, and mackerel; there is neither milk nor fruit to be had, and no butcher within some miles.

The maid-servant of our lodgings, a simple, good-natured, honest creature, who was born on this spot, and never was out of sight of the landslip, has a child; but it turned out, on inquiry, that she never had a husband; and I am informed that the landlady, a very pretty young woman, just married, has remarked on the occasion, that it was no uncommon case. She blamed the practice as *unsafe*, observing, with great appearance of simplicity, that, for her part, she thought it was much better to secure a husband first. We had much the same information in Cumberland, and in other parts of the country; and I really think the facility of American manners, about which travellers have made ill-natured remarks, has precedents here to go by.

The passage from Cowes to Southampton is 14 miles; we performed it in two hours, in a good seaboat, a sloop, of which the master was tolerably drunk; the fare only one shilling a-head, the tenth part of the toll of some of the English rivers. Spithead, full of ships at anchor, appeared at about ten miles distance. Southampton bay itself is uninteresting, the shores being low; they are well wooded, however, in many places, and diversified with gentlemen's houses. The ruins of Netley Abbey showed themselves to advantage above the trees.

July 12.—Petworth belongs to Lord E.*—a great edifice, too plain and simple for its size.

Lord E. is represented by the people of the country as a plain man, rather shy, odd, and whimsical; which is saying a great deal in a country where this disposition is common enough to escape observation. He suffers the peasants of his village to play bowls and cricket on the lawn before the house; to scribble on the walls, and even on the glass of his windows; yet he has just turned away a gardener for selling some vegetables out of a garden which might supply the country ten miles round, and I dare say does. This noblemen had a numerous family of children, the last two only legitimate; the latter died, and the title will pass to a collateral heir, with as small a portion as he can of an income of L. 80,000 a-year. There are many men in England who are libertines out of modesty, or rather *mauvaise honte*, unable to control their awe of modest women; and I understand this disposition is particularly common among the nobility. It is probably the consequence of a late university education, and being kept too long out of general society.

Of the two nights we spent at Petworth, in a very good inn, the first afforded us all the rest of which we had been deprived at Portsmouth; the second was of a very different character. There happened to be a club-dinner in the room next to us, still sitting, and rather noisy, when we went to bed. The company soon became so much more boisterous, as to destroy all hopes of sleep, and getting up, I procured a light, and took a book, but reading was also impossible. The conversation, of which very very little was lost, became more and more foolish every moment; the singing, breaking wine-glasses and chairs, and vociferating, lasted till three

---

* The 3rd Earl of Egremont (1751–1837). He did not have two legitimate children as Simond says but only one, a daughter, who was born and died in 1803. His eldest natural son, Colonel George Wyndham, later 1st Baron Leconfield, inherited Petworth and its estates; his nephew, who inherited the title, died in 1847 when the earldom became extinct.

o'clock in the morning—that is, until broad day-light—when most of these convivial gentlemen staggered home one after the other, and those remaining were too far gone to give us any farther annoyance. This scene is, I believe, quite English, though less common than formerly.

July 12.—The English boast of their humanity to animals, and may comparatively; but although animals are treated less cruelly here than in France, and are for that reason much more docile and manageable; yet there is still much to be shocked at. If you have a mind to travel with any comfort, you must not venture to look under the collars or saddles of post-horses, as you might there meet with sights to make the best post-chaise uneasy. Between Petworth and Weston-House we perceived that one of the horses was streaming with blood about the neck; he had been put in harness too soon after a bleeding. The postboy stopped on the road, and went through the operation of fresh twisting of the skin, tying, and pinning—very clumsy and painful—but unavoidable: he agreed with me that it was very wrong to work horses too soon after bleeding, *for*, said he, this is the third we have had in this situation, and the two others died of mortification, and *they cost* L. 37 *a-piece!* If you make any remark on a horse being lame or tired, they never fail to apply the whip instantly, by way of shewing the horse *can* go—something like the consequence of Don Quixote's interfering in favour of the shepherd's boy. It is a strange, but certainly a happy dispensation of providence, that the impression of these sort of things should weaken so rapidly, as soon as the object is out of sight, otherwise, as new ones presented themselves, such an accumulation of misery would at last render the situation of the traveller worse than that of his horses.

We found the inhabitants of London taken up with the splendid fête given by a young lady, sole mistress of a fortune of half a million sterling. The supper is said to have fallen rather short, and it is no wonder, for Mr Gunter (the fashionable manager of fêtes) had *only* 2000 guineas for this same supper, exclusive of lights!*

A wealthy individual, a great landholder, and a peer of the

---

* James Gunter of 7 Belgrave Square was London's most fashionable caterer and confectioner.

realm, has lately taken upon himself to sound the alarm of the depreciation in good earnest, and put it to the test; in having sent a notice to his tenants, in which he tells them that bank paper representing no longer the real value stated in their leases, he means to call upon them for payment of their rents in the legal coin of the realm; and as gold was worth L. 4 per ounce at the time these leases were granted, while its present value in the market is L. 4, 14s. in default of gold coin, he would be satisfied with paper, at the rate of L. 4, 14s. for every L. 4, or $16\frac{1}{2}$ per cent. difference, being the actual depreciation. The tenants are protected by law against the arrest of their persons, provided they tender bank notes, but are liable to be ejected from their farms; and Parliament will have to protect them further. It is undeniable that the rent agreed upon in 1804 does not represent now the same value; and that the farmer, while selling his produce at an advanced price, proportioned to the depreciation, discharges his rent at the old or reduced price—what he pays is nominal, and what he receives real. The landlord has a fair right, therefore, to come in for his share of the advanced price, and the interference of the legislature is hardly defensible on the ground of justice, although necessity may be pleaded in its favour. This is, however, to be said, that the rise of prices was in part foreseen in 1804, and that a farmer obtaining a long lease, might be induced to give a higher price than he could afford at first; in consideration of the advantages to accrue to him from the successive rise of prices during the course of his lease. It is like Esop's basket, too heavy at setting out, and too light for the latter half of the journey; but which it would not be fair to fill up again at the half-way. The zeal of the champions for the integrity of the currency, is not unlike that of the surgeon in Gil Blas, who, after wounding passengers in the street, and retreating into his house, sallied forth through another door to proffer his services, in the way of his profession.

 London is less empty than we expected, and the wheels of numerous carriages are still rattling over the pavement of Portman Square, near which we occupy the house of an absent friend, obligingly lent to us. Hyde Park is much frequented, and still green. The deer are so tame as to graze near the walks, and suffer the children to play with their horns. The swans, equally tame, come with their young ones, which are not white yet, to the margin of the Serpentine river, and take bread out of your hand.

We have in our neighbourhood one of those no-thoroughfare lanes or courts, of which Voltaire wanted to change the indelicate name they bear in French into that of *impasse*. This one is imhabited by a colony of Irish labourers, who fill every cellar and every garret—a family in each room; very poor, very uncleanly, and very turbulent. They give each other battle every Saturday night particularly, when heroes and heroines shew their prowess at fisty-cuffs, and roll together in the kennel, precisely as at Paris in the Fauxbourg St Mareau. We should never have known that there were such wretches as these in London, if we had not happened to reside in Orchard Street, Portman Square, which is one of the finest parts of the town. The uproar continued all last night, from Saturday to Sunday (5th August), and it was as impossible to sleep as at Petworth. A watchman called for assistance with his rattle. One or more of his brethren assembled; and I overheard from the window one of them say, "*If I go in I know I shall have a shower of brickbats.*" To which another replied very considerately, "*Well, never mind, let them murder each other if they please.*" This shews what sort of a mild police there is in this immense town—and yet there are as few crimes, or violence of any kind, committed here as at Paris, where the *guet-à-pied* and *guet-à-cheval* parade the streets, or at least used to do so, all night long, and even during the day, full armed. I have never heard anything similar to the noise of these neighbours of ours in any other part of the town at any hour of the night, even in St Giles's, which lies in the way to several of the playhouses.

On our return to town [from East Hackney] we stopped at Hackney, to see the ascension of a balloon. The crowd on foot and in carriages was prodigious. An uninterrupted stream poured from all the avenues towards the spot (the garden of the Mermaid publichouse), covering the whole fields, the roofs of houses, and the highest trees, like a swarm of locusts, in order to see better what could not possibly escape their sight from any place. After waiting some hours, the balloon rose at last from its hiding-place, with two

London

adventurers suspended in its gallery—Mr Sadler, a professor in that line, and Captain Paget, a candidate for fame—waving their flags.* There was a short burst of applause, then a profound silence, and some time elapsed before shouts burst again from the immense multitude. The novelty to most people, the gracefulness of the sight, and the boldness of the deed, are calculated to excite very powerful emotions, which are felt simultaneously by everybody, for a moment at least. The balloon rose nearly perpendicularly, inclining from us eastward. It was visible for 22 minutes, and in about an hour descended near Tilbury Fort; distance 30 miles.

I have already mentioned certain basins, or docks, situated below London, into which whole fleets of merchantmen are laid up under lock and key. We provided ourselves with a letter of introduction for the Captain of the West India docks, and taking a boat at the Whitehall Stairs, towards the latter part of the ebbing tide, we descended swiftly through the whole length of the town. The Adelphi and Somerset House, on the left, looked extremely well; the latter indeed magnificent, with the same black and white stains as at St Paul's, and on all other stone buildings in London; it has a singular effect, and not a bad one. The bridge opposite Somerset House is just begun; it will be only the fourth bridge, and not enough for this overgrown town. Paris has six or seven bridges. Blackfriars bridge is decaying rapidly. The stones are too soft, and scale off near the water's edge. The ornamental columns at each pier will not stand many years. It is a very handsome bridge.† Nothing can well be uglier than London bridge; every arch is of a size different from its next neighbour; there are more solid than open parts; it is in fact like a thick wall, pierced with small unequal

---

* This ascent was reported with spirit in *The Times* on 13 August 1811. William Windham Sadler was killed in a ballooning accident in 1824. His protégé, Captain Paget R.N. was presumably the Hon Sir Charles Paget, Lord Paget's brother, who was in England at this date and is the only captain of that name in the 1811 Navy List.

† This was Waterloo Bridge. Designed by John Rennie, it was finished in 1817 and demolished in 1927 to make way for the modern structure of Sir Giles Gilbert Scott. Both the Adelphi and Somerset House were relatively new; the Adam brothers having begun the Adelphi in 1772, Sir William Chambers the new Somerset House in 1775.

holes here and there, through which the current, dammed up by this clumsy fabric, rushes with great velocity, and in fact takes a leap, the difference between high and low water being upwards of 15 feet. Passengers are generally landed above, and taken up below the bridge; but being desirous of trying this little Niagara, which cannot be very dangerous, since so many boats pass it every day in safety, and being quite sure of reaching the shore by swimming, I remained with the boatman. He took the third arch, placed his boat in a direct line, then rested on his oars. The boat shot along an inclined plane, through the narrow hole, not 20 feet wide I believe—ascended a little, then descended an abrupt step—the prow straight down—and up again in a moment—lifting some water into the boat, which turned several times round in the eddy below the bridge, before it got into the straight current. I am astonished this fall, repeated twice a-day for some hours, has not undermined the bridge long ago.*

Below London Bridge, the Thames begins to assume the appearance of a sea port. You see shipping at anchor on both sides, many Dutch, Danes, and Swedes, with licenses, I suppose, and many Americans; two or three seventy-fours on the stocks, and some East Indiamen; Admiral de Winter's ship afloat, dismantled.† We soon found ourselves in a crowd of boats, very gaily attired, full of rowers, and in great activity. It was a rowing match—they appeared ready to start, and we took our station among the spectators. A shot fired was the signal. Three very light boats like the one we were in, 20 feet long—4½ feet beam—16 inches deep—the greatest breadth in the middle—sharp, fore and aft, like a shuttle—clinker built—one man in each, with sculls. One of the champions was orange all over—the other yellow—the third red. In a few minutes there was great cry of foul! foul! answered equally loud with fair! fair! The friends on both sides interfered and stopped the

---

* The houses on London Bridge, which had, for centuries, made it one of the most notable landmarks in Europe had been pulled down in the 1760's. The bridge itself was demolished in 1832 when the Rennies' granite structure, now also to be demolished, had already taken its place.

† The Dutch admiral, Jan Willem de Winter (1750–1812), had been defeated by Duncan at Camperdown in 1797.

boats. What it was exactly we could not make out, some nice point no doubt, as there was much vehement argumentation on both sides; but, apparently, without abuse or quarrelling, things were adjusted and the race resumed. The contending oarsmen passed very swiftly by us, straining every nerve, amidst shouts and acclamations. We saw them turn half-a mile above, around a large boat stationed there for the purpose, decorated with streamers, and covered with the *beau sexe* all in white. The orange man, who had the lead at first, seemed now to be overtaken by the red—the yellow far behind. Returning, they soon passed us again, on the other side, followed by a fleet of boats, and were out of sight in a few minutes, down the river—a band of music playing all the while.*

Sept. 5.—Wishing to see, or rather thinking it incumbent on me to see, something of the prisons of this capital, I called to-day at the most considerable of them, Newgate. A turnkey took me up a back stair-case to the leads, from which, like Asmodeus in the *Diable Boiteux*, I had a view of the interior, and could see what was doing in the different divisions of this melancholy abode. We first perched upon the debtors' ward—they sat and walked about in two courts, paved with flag-stones, and very clean; the women separated from the men. Some of the women, (they were few) held up their hands to me for alms. I observed written on the wall, in very large letter, *Lord Moira for ever.*† Then we went to the felons under sentence of death. They were playing fives against the wall of a narrow court; their irons fastened on one leg only, from the knee to the ankle, over a sort of cushion, and so arranged as to make no noise, and to be no impediment at all to their motions; in fact a mere matter of form—and so is also, in a great degree, the sentence of death itself. Not one of these people appeared to believe it serious. One of them, whose companions were lately executed for forgery, had been reprieved the day before, having turned evi-

---

* This was presumably Doggett's coat and badge race, an annual event founded in 1715 by Thomas Doggett, manager of Drury Lane, in honour of the accession of George I and still rowed on the Thames each July.

† Francis Rawdon-Hastings, 2nd Earl of Moira (1754–1826), subsequently became Commander-in-Chief of the forces in India. He had laboured hard to ameliorate the plight of insolvent debtors.

dence, and they were all playing with great briskness and glee. In one of the courts, the one I think for felons under sentence of transportation, I was shewn the man who fired a pistol at the king twelve or fifteen years ago, at the theatre.* He stood picking his teeth in a corner very composedly—well dressed, and looking young (he must have been quite young at the time.) I asked whether the man was insane; *Not at all*, said the turnkey, *no more than you, only very cunning.* But what is there so cunning in getting himself shut up here for life? They have made him foreman of the ward, he has a good salary—a guinea a-week, I think he said, *happy as a king—eats the best of every thing—what can he want more!* The transportation ladies, crowded in a small court, were much more disorderly than the men. They threatened and wrangled among themselves, singing, vociferating, and, as much as the narrow space allowed, moving about in all sorts of dresses—one of them in men's clothes. They are not in irons like the men. In a more spacious court, separated from these women by a high wall, were state prisoners, as my guide called them, playing fives (the favourite pastime of Newgate it seems). One of them, well dressed, and wearing powder, about forty years of age, was pointed out to me, as Astlett of the bank.† He was playing merrily with another *gentleman*, as my guide, a most vulgar wretch, called them. This other gentleman was a printer, who had been there two years for *striking for wages*, and has one or two more years to stay. Three or four years confinement in Newgate, for a confederacy of journeymen to have their wages raised, seems to me most excessive, especially as

* On 15 May 1800 the King had attended a performance of Colley Cibber's *She Would and She Would Not* at Drury Lane. While acknowledging the cheers in the front of his box, he was shot at by James Hadfield, a former soldier in the 15th Light Dragoons. Hadfield, who had been "severely wounded in the head", was tried on a charge of High Treason but was judged insane and sent to Bedlam where he died. Unless the turnkey or Simond made a mistake as to his identity it seems that for a time he must have been transferred to Newgate.

† Robert Aslett had been employed by the Bank of England for twenty-five years, and, being induced to speculate in the funds, had embezzled some £2,500 worth of securities entrusted to him. Found guilty after a lengthy trial in 1804, he was sentenced to death but afterwards reprieved. Some time after Simond's visit to Newgate he was allowed to transport himself.

their employers may confederate as much as they please among themselves for the reduction of wages. The associations of workmen, and raising a fund among themselves under certain officers, have been thought a contrivance of revolutionary tendency; and there may have been something of that sort in the present case. I inquired for Mr Cobbett, expecting to see him among the gentlemen—*Oh! no, said my turnkey, he is too great for that. Where is he then?—Why he is in the governor's house—I'll show you—plenty of money, and that is every thing you know.* Then walking farther on the leads, he shewed me a grated door, through which I could see a carpeted room—Mr Cobbett's room. He has the key of the grated door, and therefore, free access to this leaden roof, which is extensive, high, and airy, with a most beautiful view of St Paul's, and over great part of the city. His family is with him, and he continues to pour out his torrent of abuse as freely as ever, on everything and everybody in turn. Mr Cobbett seems to me to furnish, without intending it, the same sort of evidence in favour of the existence of the liberty of the press in his own country, as a philosopher of antiquity gave of the existence of motion.

The water with which London is supplied, was, it seems, conveyed by means of wooden pipes or logs, perforated, lying under ground, from which small leaden pipes branched out to each house. Workmen are now employed in taking up these logs, which appear mostly decayed, and substituting cast iron pipes. Those in the main streets, such as Oxford Street and Holborn, are enormously large; upwards of two feet diameter, branching out, down the side streets, into pipes of the diameter of six inches. The water must acquire a ferruginous quality in its passage through so much iron. I think glass pipes might be made sufficiently thick to bear moving; and once in the ground, would last for ever, and communicate no impurity to the water.

There are many native East Indians lately landed. They walk about the town with immense umbrellas, particoloured, red and white, in alternate ribs, and a deep fringe all round. Who will say now that there is no sun in London, when tropical people are obliged to screen themselves from its beams! These men, who seem to be people of some consequence, are extremely small, meagre men. It must seem to them as if they were among Patagonians, although the inhabitants of London have no particular claim to size. They are much stared at, but not insulted. An English mob is not that rude unmannerly thing it is generally taken for. It is difficult to conjecture what idea an East Indian may form, beforehand, of the mighty *company* and its august court, but I should think he must experience some surprise as he approaches the foot of his sovereign's throne, in Leaden-Hall Street.

We left London on our return to America, on Sunday the 15th September, and arrived on Wednesday evening at Liverpool, four hot and dusty days. I am convinced there is sun and blue sky enough in England to satisfy any reasonable person. We travelled by Coventry, Litchfield, Newcastle-under-Lyne [and Northwich,] 226 miles; about 20 miles more than the real distance, owing to the custom of charging one mile for a fraction of a mile at every stage.

We passed some very showy barracks, built of freestone, at a vast expence, with many subdivisions, and enclosed with high walls. The Romans had no such establishments for their army—mud huts, and a ditch, and all done by the soldiers themselves; who, thus trained and employed, bore fatigue and hardships, that now destroy more men than the sword, in a British army particularly, I believe. The men loiter or lie about in the shade—neat and good-looking, but very ill prepared for a campaign in Portugal. This applies also to their cavalry. The horses are certainly handsome—high fed, and pampered—their charge is spirited and powerful: but every body says they are much sooner knocked up than the small, lean cattle of the French cavalry.

From Newcastle-under-Lyne, we went two miles out of our way to visit Etruria, the famous manufactory of earthen ware, founded by Wedgwood and Bentley, about fifty years ago. The clay is ground by means of screws *sans fin* passing through certain frames of the shape of funnels, and by other processes; then washed in a quantity of water, which carries away the finest parts only, obtained afterwards by the evaporation of the water. Flints calcined and pulverized are worked in the same manner. These substances, mixed together in certain proportions, determined by the kind of ware intended to be made, form a paste, which is modelled and shaped by skilful hands. The neat, strong, light, and beautiful ware, known all over Europe by the name of Wedgwood, need not be described. This is not, however, a simple manufactory of plates and dishes: Mr Bentley, one of its founders, was a man of taste, and had travelled in Italy. He introduced the classical forms of antique vases, as much as these could be applied to real use in these modern times. He also imitated, with great success, the fine ornamental vases of Greece and Rome, as well as antique cameos.

To form an idea of the vast extent of these works, it is enough to know that the force of a steam-engine, of eighty horse power, is requisite to set the whole in motion, and overcome the inertia of so much clay and water. You see but few workmen besides those employed in modelling the clay. All such processes as require the mere exertion of force regularly and uniformly applied, are performed by various machines, all receiving their first impulse from the steam-engine. The unerring exactness and power, ever equal to a given end, of these creations of human intelligence, never fail to produce in me a lively feeling of admiration and enthusiasm, which I may have expressed before, although not half so often as it has been felt.

The coating of the Wedgwood ware was originally, I believe, composed of calx of lead, silex, and pounded glass. This glazing being in some degree soluble by acids, might be dangerous to health; and I believe the lead is now totally excluded from its composition. These substances, with the addition, I believe, of some soda, are ground in water to the consistency of cream. The vase, already baked, is dipped into the liquor, which penetrates its pores, and leaves in them, and on the surface, by drying up, an extremely fine powder, which is afterwards vitrified by exposure to heat, and partly incorporated in the substance of the ware. The flowers, and other coloured ornaments, are applied by the hands of female artists generally, and with much dexterity and quickness.

A *private* canal receives the produce of the manufactory at the very door, and conveys it to the great junction canal, by which labour and breakage are saved.

When I remember the common-ware used in France, coarse and heavy, with the glazing scaling off, or full of cracks crossing each other in every direction, like lace-work, and retaining in their interstices the various juices of a hundred successive dinners, the vulgar blue border carried all round an awkward scolloped edge, it seems to me as if the useful arts had been then comparatively in their infancy.

The county of Cheshire, which we have last traversed, is famed for its salt-works and its cheeses. The salt-springs, with which it abounds, were used by the inhabitants long before they understood the art of making salt by evaporation and crystallization; for we find Henry VI inviting Dutchmen to come over and instruct his barbarous subjects in that simple art. The discovery of the beds of fossil, or rock-salt, is of a much more recent date; the first was found in 1670, at the depth of 34 yards, in searching for coals near Northwich. The bed was 30 yards in thickness. This discovery occasioned new researches; and the same bed was discovered to extend all over the immediate neighbourhood. In 1779, a new bed, or stratum of salt, was discovered near Lawton, 15 or 20 miles to the southeast of the first mines, at the depth of 42 yards, four feet thick only. Beneath the salt, was a stratum of indurated clay of 10 yards; then a second bed of salt of four yards; then 15 yards of the same clay; and, finally, a third bed of salt, through which they penetrated to the depth of 24 yards, when, finding that the centre of the bed, forming about 14 yards, was of a purer quality than the parts above or below, they stopped there. This experiment encouraged the miners of Northwich to look deeper for purer salt; and, in 1781, they penetrated to a new stratum of salt, 40 yards in thickness, separated from the old one by a stratum of indurated clay of 10 yards. The centre of this new bed of salt was found to be much more free from earthy particles; and it has been worked ever since. We descended into this mine. My companions, dressed in the costume of the place, a flannel over-all, were seated in a large tub, suspended by a rope; one of the miners stood on the edge, to keep the tub steady in its descent. At the depth of 330 feet, we found ourselves in a sort of palace of salt. The ceiling, about 20 feet high, was supported by pillars 15 feet thick, at very bold, and, I should think, alarming distances, considering the prodigious weight above. I measured 53 steps (159 feet) between some of them!

The rent of cottages varies in this county from L. 4 to L. 9; the lowest have a small garden, the highest land sufficient for the keep of a cow. This practice, of attaching a small portion of land to the cottages of labourers, is often deprecated as injurious. The disadvantage of small farms cannot be doubted; they require, in a great degree, the same implements and stock as large ones—do not admit of a proper division of labour—and of a steady and regular employment of time. But the few acres of the cottager require, on the other hand, no stock, and take up only such leisure hours, or days, as he can spare from his regular calling, while his young family are furnished with an employment fitted to their strength. It would not answer as a main dependance, but is a valuable auxiliary.

I was struck with the following ingenious method of constructing covered drains, by means of bricks, 9 inches long, 6 wide, and $3\frac{1}{4}$ inches in thickness. On one of the sides is pressing in, at making the bricks, half a cylindrical piece of wood, of 3 inches in diameter. Two bricks of this form, laid face to face, leave of course a circular hole of three inches between them for the passage of water, and placed end to end at the bottom of a ditch, and, covered with earth, form a permanent drain, not liable to go out of order.

Money, for want of employment, bears a low interest; good notes at six months can be discounted at $2\frac{1}{2}$ per cent.; hence Government finds little difficulty in filling loans, and the same cause fills the army and navy. Commercial distress is felt more severely in manufacturing towns. A single house of Manchester discharged last Saturday 1200 workmen; another 500! These poor people must live—and in some parishes the poor-rates are already 6s. in the pound! Live they *may* certainly, for there is not less food in the country. The rich will have to pay them to be soldiers, or to do nothing, instead of paying for the luxuries imported from foreign countries, in exchange for articles of home manufactures.

We have visited the asylum for the blind; a most humane establishment, by which a number of unfortunate individuals are made happy by employment and independence. They learn a trade— are supported for three or four years—and dismissed with a little fund. They weave cloth very well, make neat pretty baskets, elegant rugs for fire-places, bed-side carpets &c. &c. and some of them are good musicians. They give weekly concerts, and the correctness, vigour, and expression of their singing are surprising. There were some fine voices, and the organ was played by the blind. Unconscious of *looks*, and totally unable to modulate their features, the expression of their countenances had no guide but inward feelings, which lead them right in some instances, and wrong in others. We observed some of the women smiling sweetly at each other; and at other times, but mostly the men, making hideous grimaces, with odd uncouth attitudes and gestures, particularly when singing. Some of these poor people, traversing a court to go to dinner, turned to the sun, looking up to it, much pleased with *seeing* some glimmering of light. I asked one of the women how long it was since she had lost her sight? Since she was a year old, she said. "You have of course no idea of what light is; you do not think of it, I suppose." "Indeed I do but too much!" Others declared they cared very little about it.

Sept. 25, 1811.—We are waiting only for a change of wind to go on board the ship which is to carry us away, for ever perhaps, from a country, where we have been received with kindness, and where we leave a few friends. There is a seriousness in the thought—and the near prospect of a long voyage, and all its hazards, is not likely to dissipate the gloom. If I was asked, at this moment, for a summary opinion of what I have seen in England, I might probably say that its political institutions present a detail of corrupt practices—of profusion—and of personal ambition, under the mask of public-spirit very carelessly put on, more disgusting than I should have expected: the workings of the selfish passions are exhibited in all their nakedness and deformity. On the other hand, I should admit very readily, that I have found the great mass of the people richer, happier, and more respectable, than any other with which I am acquainted. I have seen prevailing among all ranks of people that emulation of industry and independence which characterize a state of advancing civilization, properly directed. The manners, and the whole deportment of superiors to inferiors, are marked with that just regard and circumspection which announce the presence of laws equal for all. By such signs I know this to be the best government that ever existed. I sincerely admire it in its results, but I cannot say I particularly like the means. What I dislike here, I might be told, belongs to human nature in general; to the world, rather than to England particularly. It may be so—and I shall not undertake the panegyric of either one or the other.

The government of England is eminently practical. The one under which I have lived many years might be defined, on the contrary, a government of abstract principles.

The lower people in England hold other nations in thorough contempt. The same rank in France, in the interior of the country at least, scarcely know there are other nations—their geography is that of the Chinese.

Of all the various merits claimed by the proud Islanders, I believe none is less disputed than that of generosity. It is not only a received thing that an Englishman has always plenty of money and gives it away very freely, but no sacrifice of a higher kind is supposed to be above his magnanimity. I have to remark on this subject that those who give a little, after promising much, appear to have given nothing, while those who, without promising any thing, give a little, have credit on the contrary for giving a great deal. This accounts, in part, for the two opposite reputations, the one for unmeaning politeness and mere show of sentiments, the other for simple and blunt generosity. The fact is, as to giving substantially, that it is much easier for the English to do than the French, and accordingly much more is given in money by the former than by the latter; but I doubt extremely whether the English are more disposed than their neighbours to bestow their time and personal attention upon their friends in sickness or misfortune, and upon the distressed in general. There is in England a sort of fastidious delicacy, coldness, or pride, which stands a good deal in the way of active benevolence. The ties of blood are also, I think, weaker in France. People seem to calculate with more strictness how far the claim of kindred extends, and even the highest degree of consanguinity, that of parents and children, seems to command rather less deference and respect. A cousin may certainly not be more to you than another man, yet it is an amiable error, and a useful one, to think yourself obliged to show some kindness, and feel some particular sympathy for the man, whom nature has placed nearly in the same rank of life with yourself, and whom you are likely to meet oftenest in your journey through life.

The English are better reasoners than the French, and therefore more disposed to be just—the first of moral qualities; and yet the propensity to luxury and ostentation is so strong, as well as so general here, as to expose this same sense of justice to hard trials. I never knew a prodigal who was just, nor indeed truly generous—he never has it in his power.

I do not conceive it possible for some of the most horrible scenes of the French Revolution to be acted here, in any event. The people in France are capable of greater atrocities than those of England, but I should think the latter sterner—less prone to cruelty, but less susceptible of pity.

Upon the whole, I believe the national differences to have less reality than appearance. The same vices, and the same virtues—the same propensities and views, under very different forms, are found in both countries, more nearly alike than is generally supposed.

Index

Abercrombie, Alexander (1784–1852) 145–6, 146 n.
Abercrombie, Sir Ralph 145, 146 n.
Aberystwyth 67
Adam, James (1730–94) 157 n.
Adam, Robert (1728–92) 27 n., 157 n.
Agriculture, in Norfolk, 57–8; in North of England, 71; in Scotland, 75; harvesting, 81; in West Riding, 111; and industrial revolution, 144; on Isle of Wight, 152; *see also* Farming
Albury 146–7
Aliens, registration of 60
Alnwick, 103; castle, 103–4, 104 n.
Amelia, Princess (1783–1810) 124 n.
Anglesey, Henry William Paget, 1st Marquess of (1768–1854) 97–8, 97 n.
Anstruther, Sir John 42
Aranda, Pedro Pablo Abarca y Bolea, Count of (1718–99) 94–5, 94 n.
Argyll, George Campbell, 6th Duke of (d. 1841) 97 n., 98
Artificial limbs 47
Aslett, Robert 160 and n.
Assemblies in London, 31; in Edinburgh, 89
Astley, Philip (1742–1814) 130 and n.

Balloon ascent 156–7
Bangor Ferry 67, 68
Banks, Sir Joseph 43
Bannister, John (1760–1836), 93–4, 93 n.
Barnsley 113
Barracks 162
Barrows 58
Barry, Edward M. 45 n.
Bath 19–20

Baths 118
Beaufort, Duke of 65
Beggars 18, 26, 58
Belcher, Jim 48 and n.
Bentley, T. 162, 163
Birmingham, 122; manufacture in, 118–21
Blenheim Palace 122–3
Blind asylum 165–6
Boat race 158–9
Bodmin 17
Book clubs 59
Botany Bay, transportation to 50, 89
Boxing *see* Pugilism
Braham, John (1774–1856) 93 and n.
Brewery, Barclay's 132–3
Bristol 18, 64, 65
British Museum, 44 n.; Simond's visit to, 43–4
Brown, Lancelot ("Capability" Brown, 1715–83) 104 and n.
Bonaparte, Napoleon (1769–1821), divorce and remarriage, 15 and n.; and rockets, 41 n.
Burdett, Sir Francis (1770–1844), 38 and n., 54; imprisoned in the Tower, 41–2; petition for his release, 42–3
Burlington, Richard Boyle, 3rd Earl of (1695–1753) 128
Bury St Edmunds 58

Cambridge, the University Library 59
Campbell, Colen (d. 1729), 26; builds Stourhead, 64 n.
Canals 71, 163
Cardiff 66, 67
Carlisle 71
Carnarvon 67

Carriages, 65; in Falmouth, 14; post-chaises, 16, 21; to assemblies in London, 30, 31; in Edinburgh, 86
Carts 75, 85
Castle Howard 110
Castleton 113
Catalini, Angelica (1779–1849) 44 and n.
Chambers, Sir William (1726–96) 157 n.
Charles XII, King of Sweden (1682–1718) 59
Chatsworth 116–17, 128
Chepstow 65, 66
Cheshire, cheese and salt from 164
Child labour, in cotton mills, 77, 78; wages, 77; health, 77–8; in coal mines, 105
Chester, the court-house and prison, 69; architecture of, 70
Chiswick House 128
Church, poor attendance at, 61, 134; Scots country people attend, 80
Clarence, Duke of (later King William IV, 1765–1837) 145
Clarke, Dr Edward Daniel 59 and n.
Cloth trade, the 112
Coal mining 105–7
Cobbett, William (1763–1855), and Burdett, 42 and n.; tried for libel, 64–5, 65 n.; in Newgate, 161
Cobbett's Political Register 66
Coleridge, Samuel Taylor (1772–1834) 83–4, 83 n.
Congreve rockets 40–1
Congreve, Sir William (1772–1828) 41 n.
Cook, Captain James (1728–79) 107
Cooke, George Frederick (1756–1811) 46 and n.
Copper and iron works, operations in 67
Cottages see Houses
Cotton mills 77, 78
Cowbridge 66
Cowes 151, 152
Cribb, Tom (1781–1848) 48 and n.
Criminal trial 86–91
Cromwell, Oliver (1599–1658) 66
Crow Castle 68
Cumberland, Duke of (1771–1851) 53 and n.
Currency, depreciation of 154–5
Custom-house, business at 13, 15
Customs, an English dinner 34–6

Deaths, in Lake District 82, 83
Deer, at Wilton, 62; in Blenheim Park, 123; in Hyde Park, 156
Deshayes, André-Jean (1777–1864) 44 and n.
Devonshire, William Cavendish, 6th Duke of (1790–1858), and Chatsworth, 117 and n.; and Chiswick House, 128
de Winter, Admiral Jan Willem (1750–1812), 158 and n.
Dinas Bran 68
Doggett, Thomas (d. 1721), the "Coat and Badge" race 158–9, 159 n.
Drainage, in London, 37; primitive conditions in Scotland, 75; lack of, in Edinburgh, 94; in Madrid, 94–5; ditch drainage, 165
Dress, of men, 14, 111; of women, 14, 54, 111; of Scotsmen, 75, 80; of Scotswomen, 75, 77; of judges, 86, 108, 111; of prisoners of war, 95; of Oxford students, 124; of clerks of the House, 137; of women after the Prince Regent's fête, 148 n, 149; of salt miners, 164
Drought 54
Dunkeld 80

East India Company 143
East Indians 161–2
Edinburgh, 81, 85, 98; description of, 76; penitentiary house in, 76; weather in, 77; the fish market, 77; amusements and way of life in, 89; hogmanay in, 90; Fox anniversary dinner in, 90–3; filth of, 94; Castle, 95
Egremont, 3rd Earl of (1751–1837) 153 and n.
Elizabeth I, Queen (1533–1603) 145
Elliston, Robert William (1774–1831) 138–9, 138 n.
Epping Forest 143
Erskine, Henry (1746–1817) 91 and n., 92
Espriella, Manuel Alvarez see Southey, Robert
Executions at Chester 69
Exeter, 15; Cathedral, 17 and n.

Falmouth, the harbour, 13; the hotel at, 14; lodgings in, 16; countryside surrounding, 16

Index

Farmers, 111; financial position of, 98–9; and depreciation of currency, 155
Farming, in Devon, 18; in Surrey, 50–1; in Norfolk, 58; in Northumberland, 103; and the economy, 144; on Isle of Wight, 152; *see also* Agriculture
Fawcett, John (1768–1837) 129 and n.
Ferries, Conway, 68; Liverpool, 70; Southampton, 152
Fingall, 8th Earl of (1759–1831) 91 n., 92
Firth of Forth 79
Fish market 77
Fishing and fishing tackle 151–2
Fishwives 77
Fitzgerald, William 39 and n.
Flint glass manufacture 119–20
Flushing 13
Food, at Falmouth hotel, 14, 15; milk delivery in London, 30; an English dinner, 34; of Highland peasants, 79, 80; of prisoners of war, 95; in House of Commons, 138; on Isle of Wight, 152
Fox, Charles James (1749–1806), the anniversary dinner on birthday of, 90–3, 91 n.; and Chiswick House, 128
Frazer, Lieutenant-Colonel Sir Augustus 41
Frenchmen, caricatured 28
Funeral 97
Furniture, tables, 34; commodes, 35–6; in Highland dwellings, 79

Gas lighting 119–20
George Prince Regent (later King George IV, 1762–1830), 146; his fête, 148
George III (1738–1820), his birthday celebrations, 53–4, 53 n.; at Windsor Castle, 124 and n.; and the Prince Regent's fête, 148
Giant 60
Gillies, Adam (1760–1842), 90–1, 91 n.
Glasgow 78
Gothic style, the 151
Grasmere 82
Grattan, Henry (1746–1820) 39 and n.
Greenwich Hospital 51–2

Gregan-Craufurd, Sir Charles 39 and n.
Grenville, Lord George 39 and n.
Gretna Green 85–6
Guards, march to Hyde Park, 30; Life Guards and London rioters, 42
Gully, John (1783–1863) 48 and n.
Gunter, James 154 and n.
Gypsies 122

Hackney 156
Hackney coaches, 26; in Edinburgh, 86
Hadfield, James, 160 and n.
Haileybury College 143–4, 143 n.
Hamilton, the Duke of 78
Hamlet, the grave-diggers 129–30
Hatfield House 145
Hawick 71
Haystacks 103, 111
Health of copper and iron workers, 67; of child labourers, 77–8; of Highlanders, 79; of coal miners, 107; goitre, 118; and manufactories, 118; and potteries, 163
Hertford 145
Hoare, Henry 64 n.
Hoare, Sir Richard 63
Hogs 80
Home, Countess of, Adam designs 20 Portman Square for 27
Horses, post horses, 16, 20, 67; in Devon, 18; size of London horses, 29; in agriculture, 57, 58, 67, 111; quality of, 64; cost of hiring, 68; taxes on, 81; in coal mines, 105, 106, 107; scarcity of, 113; in stage performances, 130, 134; at Barclay's Brewery, 132, 133; at review on Wimbledon Common, 146; ill-treatment of, 154; cavalry horses, 162
Hospitals, Simond's visit to, 39–40; Leeds Infirmary, 112–13
Hotels and Inns, at Falmouth, 14; at Ivy Bridge, 17; in Bristol, 18; The White Hart, Bath, 19; comfort of, 21; near Anglesey, 67; Liverpool Arms, 70; Dunbreck's, Edinburgh, 86; in Leeds, 112; at Barnsley, 113; at Matlock, 118; fisherman's cottage on Isle of Wight, 151; at Petworth, 153–4;

House of Commons, Simond visits, 38–9, 136–8; Burdett and, 41; committee on manufacturers' grievances in, 144–5
Houses and cottages; gentlemen's houses in Cornwall, 17; Devon village houses, 18; in Lincoln's Inn Fields, 26 and n.; London houses, 36–7, 127; in Surrey countryside, 51; in Norfolk, 58; of Sir Richard Hoare, 63 and n.; on the way to Bristol, 64; in Wales, 66; Westmorland cottages, 71; Highland dwellings, 79; on coal-mining land, 107; in Sheffield, 113; in Peak's Hole, 113; in Derbyshire, 117; in Warwickshire, 122; in Oxfordshire, 122; Edinburgh houses, 127; on outskirts of London, 142–3; cottages near Southampton, 150; Gothic thatched cottage at Cowes, 151
Howard, John (1726–90), and Chester prison, 69 and n.; and Leeds Infirmary, 112–13
Hume, David (1711–76) 43
Hunt, James Henry Leigh (1784–1859) 129 n, 138 n.
Hygiene, 35, 36; in Edinburgh, 94

Industrial revolution, 144–5; and the cloth workers, 112
Influenza 29
Inns *see* Hotels and Inns
Insanity 110, 151
Irish labourers 156
Iron foundries 118–19
Isle of Wight, 151; agriculture on, 152
Ivy Bridge 17

Jackson, John (1769–1845) 49 and n.
Jeffrey, Francis Jeffrey (1773–1850), 88 and n.
Johnson, Dr Samuel (1709–84), on unhygienic behaviour of the French, 36 n.; and Thrale's Brewery, 133 and n.
Jones, Inigo (1573–1652), and Lindsey House, 26; and Wilton House, 61
Jurymen, selection of, 86–7; attentiveness of 89

Kean, Edmund (c. 1789–1833) 46 n.
Kemble, Charles (1775–1854), 46 and n.; as *Hamlet*, 129
Kendal 70
Kent, Edward, Duke of (1767–1820) 132
Killin 79

Labourers 82
Lamb, Charles (1775–1834) 129 n.
Lamps, in London streets 30, 127
Lanark 77, 78
Lancaster, Joseph (1778–1838), 130; his school, 131–2
Langdale 82
Lansdown, William Petty, 1st Marquess of (1737–1805) 150–1, 151 n.
Lauderdale, James Murray, 8th Earl of (1759–1839) 91 n., 92
Lawns, 51; at Wilton House, 62; at Stourhead, 63
Lawton, salt mining at 164
Leasowes, the 121–2
Leeds 111–13
Leith 95
Liston, Sir Robert (1742–1836) 94 and n.
Liverpool, 162; compared with New York, 70; John Wesley's opinion of, 70 n.
Llangollen 69
London, dinginess of, 25; its squares, 26; a simple geography of, 27; in the morning, 29–30; fashionable life in, 30–1; fashionable and unfashionable sides of, 32; weather in, 33–4; the vastness of, 127; increasing spread of, 142–3; water supply of, 161
 Adelphi, the 157 and n.
 Astley's Theatre 130 n., 134
 Bishopsgate Street 27
 Blackfriars Bridge 157
 Bond Street 30, 133
 Carlton House 32 n., 149
 City, the 31, 32
 Cornhill 27
 Covent Garden Opera House, 45 and n.; *Hamlet* at, 129
 Downing Street 32
 Guildhall 136
 Haymarket Theatre 138
 Holborn 27

Index

Hyde Park 64, 155–6
Hyde Park Corner 25
Leadenhall Street 162
Lincoln's Inn Fields 26
Liverpool Museum 139
London Bridge 157–8, 157 n.
Marylebone Park 32 n.
Newgate 159–61
Orchard Street 156
Oxford Street 27
Parliament House 32
Piccadilly 27 and n.
Portman Square 27, 155, 156
Regent Street 32 n.
St Giles's 156
St James's Palace 54
St Paul's Cathedral 25, 27, 108
Serpentine, the 64, 156
Soho Square 32
Somerset House 157 and n.
Strand, the 27
Temple Bar 135
Tower, the, Burdett imprisoned in, 41, 42; description of, 135; menagerie at, 135–6
Treasury, the 32
Waterloo Bridge 157 and n.
Westminster 32
Westminster Abbey, 108, 128–9, lions of, 134; waxworks at, 135
Whitehall Stairs 157
Londoners, their civility, 28; their appearance, 28–9

Maghee, Colonel 95
Magna Charta 44
Manners, 166; of the populace to strangers, 28; of Scots country people, 80; of Northumberland children, 104–5; of Birmingham factory workers, 120–1; of the Prince Regent, 149
Manners, General 124
Marlborough, John Churchill, 1st Duke of (1650–1722) 122
Marriage, in Scotland, 85–6; in England, 85
Massena, André, Marshal (1758–1817) 130 n.
Matlock 117–18
Melrose 81
Menageries, itinerant, in Edinburgh, 93; at Tower of London, 135–6
Militia see Troops

Milk-women 29–30
Moira, Francis Rawdon-Hastings, 2nd Earl of (1754–1826) 159 and n.
Molesey Hurst 140
Molineaux, Tom 140–2
Mouse, river 78
Munden, Joseph Shepherd (1758–1832) 129 and n.
Music, 145; at Edinburgh routs, 89; in York Minster, 109; *Black-ey'd Susan*, 116; in Westminster Abbey, 128; fisherman's songs on Isle of Wight, 151; in Blind asylum, 166

Nasmyth, Patrick (1787–1831) 91–2, 91 n.
Nelson, Horatio, Viscount Nelson (1758–1805), 136; his effigy in Westminster Abbey, 135
Netley Abbey 153
Newby Hall 107–8
Newcastle, 104; coal mining at, 105
New Forest 143, 150
Newmarket, country round about 57
Newport, Isle of Wight 151
Newport, Monmouthshire 66
Newton, Charles Hay, Lord (d. 1811), 91 n., 92
Northwich, salt mining at 164
Novosielsky, Michael 45 n.

Ormskirk 70
Oxborough 57
Oxford 124

Paget, Captain the Hon. Sir Charles 157 and n.
Paget, Lady (formerly Lady Caroline Elizabeth Villiers) 97 n., 98
Paget, Lord see Anglesey, Marquess of
Palladio, Andrea (1518–80) 128
Panizzi, Antonio (later Sir Anthony, 1797–1879) 44 n.
Panoramae, exhibition of 139
Parties see Assemblies
Paxton, Sir Joseph (1801–65) 117 n.
Peak's Hole 113–15
Pembroke, 11th Earl of (1759–1827) 61, 62 n.

Penal code, the English, 49 and n., 50; the pillory, 83; trial of witches by immersion, 85 and n.
Pendennis Castle 13
Percival, Spencer (1762–1812) 137
Petty, Sir William (1623–87) 60–1, 61 n.
Petworth House 153–4
Place, Francis 53 n.
Planta, Joseph 44 n.
Plymouth 17
Police, of London, 29, 156; and violence, 50; in Scotland, 90
Politics, 166; criticism of government, 32–3, 33 n.; subject of mealtime conversation, 35; provincial attitudes to, 64, 65
Population, Petty's estimate of increase in, 60–1; 61 n.; of Edinburgh, 76
Porchester, Lord 39 and n.
Postilions, their charge 68
Prices, of lodgings, 16, 86; of houses, 19, 37, 76–7; of meat, 19, 58; of Bath hotel, 19; of tips, 19, 123, 136; of groceries, 37; of animals, 37, 38; of maintaining Greenwich pensioners, 52; of bread, 58, 148; of book-clubs, 59; farm rents, 65; of hiring horses, 68; charges on ferries, 68, 70, 152; annual expenditure in Edinburgh, 77; of whisky, 80; rent of Highland huts, 81; of land in Lake District, 82; of meals in lodgings, 86; cost of maintaining prisoners of war, 96; of estates, 99, 148; rent of coal mines, 105; of the Newby Hall *Venus*, 108; of cloth, 112; poor rate, 117, 148, 165; of gas lighting, 120; fees of guides at Blenheim, 123; of Oxford guide book, 124; values at Barclay's brewery, 132, 133; of boxes for the opera, 133; and corruption in Irish schools, 136; of Haileybury College fees, 143; of oak trees, 148; rent of meadows and farm land, 148; cost of Prince Regent's fête, 148 n.; cost of building Southampton Castle, 151 n.; of horses 154; of a supper party, 154
Prisoners of war 95–7, 149, 150
Prisons, Chester, 69; Edinburgh, 76; full, in York, 111; Newgate, 159–61
Pugilism 48–9, 140–2

Quakers, and Sunday Observance Act, 14; and the lunatic asylum near York, 109–10; West's picture for, 129 n.

Raglan Castle 65–6
Rennie, John (1761–1821) 157 n.
Richmond, 25, 127; the view from Richmond Hill, 128
Rimmer, the Lancashire boxer 140–2
Roads, outside Falmouth, 16; composition of, 18, 85, 105, 122; condition of, 20, 64; in Norfolk, 58
Romilly, Sir Samuel (1757–1818) 49 and n.
Rose, George 39 and n.
Rosetta Stone, the 43
Ross-on-Wye 65
Routs *see* Assemblies
Ruthven 68

Sadler, William Windham (d. 1824) 157 and n.
Salvin, Anthony (1799–1881) 104 n.
Salisbury 61
Salisbury, Marquis of 145
Salt mines 164
Schools, in the Highlands, 80; Lancaster's, 131–2; Irish schools discussed in Parliament, 136
Scott, Sir Giles Gilbert (1880–1960) 157 n.
Scott, Sir Walter (1771–1832) appearance and personality 90
Sedan chairs, in Falmouth, 14; ladies carried to Court in, 54; in Edinburgh, 86
Sellis, valet of Duke of Cumberland 53 and n.
Servants, 19; at Falmouth hotel, 14, 15; at Bath hotel, 19; London maidservants, 30; London footmen, 30; their quarters, 36; wages of, 37–8; scarcity of, 82; at Chatsworth, 116; at the Leasowes, 121; at Blenheim, 123; at Hatfield, 145; maidservant in Isle of Wight, lodging, 152

Index

Sheep, in Norfolk, 58; in parks, 62; in Scotland, 75; in the Highlands, 79, 80; in West Riding, 111; sheep farming and the economy, 144; sheep-shearing, 147; on Isle of Wight, 152
Sheffield 113
Shenstone, William (1714-63) 121 and n.
Shops, in Bath, 20; in London, 25, 28; in Edinburgh, 76
Siddons, Sarah (1755-1831) 46 and n.
Simond, Louis (1767-1831), his history 8-9
Smirke, Sir Robert (1781-1867) 44 n., 45 n.
Smith, Sydney (1771-1845) 109, 110
Snakes 68
Soane, Sir John (1753-1837) 26 n.
Southampton, 150, 152-3; Southampton Castle, 150-1
Southey, Robert (1774-1843) 83 n., 120 and n.
Speedwell lead-mine 114-16
Stage coaches, 21, 111; from Richmond to London, 25; London-Bath, 26-7; construction of, 81
Steam engines, in cotton mills, 78; in coal mines, 106; in iron foundry, 118; in Wedgwood works, 163
Stourhead 62-4
Surrey 50-1
Swansea 67

Tan-y-Bwlch 67
Tarleton, General Sir Banastre (1754-1833) 39 n.
Taunton 17
Taxes, 77; income-tax, 33 n.; hearth-tax, 81; window-tax, 81; on horses, 81; on whisky, 81; burden of, 82; in manufactories, 119
Tay, river 79
Taymouth 80
Tenby 67
Thames, river, 27; frozen over, 90; below London Bridge, 158
Theatres, 45 n., 46 n.; behaviour in, 45-6; in Edinburgh, 93-4; sale of boxes at opera, 133
Tilbury Fort 157
Tories 32
Towneley, Charles (1737-1805) 43

Trade Unions 33 n.
Transportation 49, 89, 160
Trees, in Surrey, 50, 51, 148; plantations near Newmarket, 57; in Wilton park, 62; at Stourhead, 63-4; at Valle Crucis Abbey, 69; marking the Border, 71; timber felling in Derbyshire, 117; in Oxfordshire, 122; in spring, 127-8; cedars at Chiswick House, 128; in Southampton, 150
Tring 85
Troops, in Bristol, 65; exercising at Ormkirk, 70; at review on Wimbledon Common, 146
Turnbull, Rev. Dr Alexander (1748-1831) 90, 91 n.
Twickenham 128

Ullswater 81
Undercliff 151

Vale of Monmouth 65
Vale of Usk 65
Valle Crucis Abbey 68-9
Vestris, Armand (1787-1825) 44-5 and n.

Wages, of hotel servants, 19; of domestic servants, 37-8, 77; labour, 58; of copper and iron workers, 67; for child labour, 77; of Highlanders, 79, 80; of colliers, 107; of cloth workers, 112; of Birmingham factory workers, 120; of foreman of the ward in Newgate, 160
Waggons, English 75, 85
Walcheren expedition, the unpopularity of, 16 and n.; discussed in Parliament, 38-9
Wallace, Sir William (c. 1274-1305) 78
Walpole, Horace, 4th Earl of Orford (1717-97) 150
Warwick 122
Watchmen 156
Water closets 37
Weather, 81, 116; fog in Corwall, 17; in London, 33-4, 161-2; the temperate climate, 65, 67, 68; and domestic architecture, 70; continual rain in Edinburgh, 77;

Weather – *cont.*
  mild, 90, 111; snowstorm, 93; a cold spring, 127; Simond's opinion of, 162
Weddell, William (1725–92) 108 n.
Wedgwood, Josiah (1730–95), founds Etruria works 162
Wedgwood works 162–3
Wellesley, Henry, later 1st Baron Cowley (1773–1847) 97 n.
Wellesley, Lady Charlotte, divorce and remarriage 97–8, 97 n.
Wellington, Arthur Wellesley, 1st Duke of (1769–1852), 16 n., 130 n.; prejudiced against rockets, 41 n.
Wesley, John (1703–91) 71
West, Benjamin (1738–1820) 129
Weston 51
Whigs, 32; Coleridge, Southey and Wordsworth and, 84
Whisky, 80; taxed, 81
Whitbread, Samuel (1758–1815) 137
Wilberforce, William (1759–1833), appearance and bearing 136–7
Wilton House 61–2, 62 n.
Wimbledon Common 146
Winchester 149, 150

Windermere 81
Windham, William (1750–1810), 49–50 and n.; his death and reputation, 52–3
Windmills 103
Windsor Castle 124
Witches 85 and n.
Women, appearance of, Welsh, 67; Lancashire, 70; Westmorland, 71; Scots, 77, 80; Northumberland, 104
Woodstock 122
Wordsworth, William (1770–1850) 83–4
Wren, Sir Christopher (1632–1723) 52 n.
Wyatt, James (1746–1813), and Wilton House, 62 n.; and Windsor Castle, 124 n.; and Chiswick House, 128 n.
Wyatville, Sir Jeffrey (1766–1840), 62 n., 117 n.; and Windsor Castle, 124 n.
Wyndham, Colonel George 153 n.

York, 107; the Minster, 108, 128; the assizes, 108–9; Quaker lunatic asylum near, 109–10